快乐从此刻开始

（汉英对照）

Happiness begins at this moment

董　雯◎著

四川科学技术出版社

·成都·

图书在版编目（CIP）数据

快乐从此刻开始:汉英对照 / 董雯著. – 成都:
四川科学技术出版社, 2019.3
ISBN 978-7-5364-9397-1

Ⅰ.①快… Ⅱ.①董… Ⅲ.①英语–汉语–对照读物
Ⅳ.①H319.4

中国版本图书馆 CIP 数据核字(2019)第 041024 号

快乐从此刻开始（汉英对照）

著　　者	董　雯
出 品 人	钱丹凝
责任编辑	刘涌泉
责任校对	王国芬
封面设计	景秀文化
责任出版	欧晓春
出版发行	四川科学技术出版社
	成都市槐树街 2 号　邮政编码 610031
	官方微博:http://e.weibo.com/sckjcbs
	官方微信公众号:sckjcbs
	传真:028–87734039
成品尺寸	145mm×210mm
	印张 5.25　字数 120 千　插页 2
印　　刷	四川科德彩色数码科技有限公司
版　　次	2019 年 3 月第一版
印　　次	2019 年 3 月第一次印刷
定　　价	39.80 元

ISBN 978-7-5364-9397-1

序 言
Preface

　　曾几何时，我不再思考我的人生，只想平凡度过一生，安逸就是我的追求。或许，每个人的一生都是不同的，人们有不同的经历、不同的生活方式。每个人的人生都不相同，我们可以自己选择。人的一生会经历成功与失败、快乐与忧伤、顺利与挫折。正因为有这样的经历，才让我们的人生丰富多彩。

　　每个人的一生都会经历很多刻骨铭心的事，正因为挫折，让我们学会了成长，学会了战胜困难。如果我们的人生只有快乐，就缺少了战胜痛苦的能力，那么还如何能体会出快乐？人的一生会面临很多困境，在困境中我们长大了，成熟了，体验到了快乐。

　　人生苦短，但不可荒废。对于20世纪60年代末出生的我来说，6岁以前都是无忧无虑的童年，之后便是15年的小学、初中、高中和大学读书时光。由于大四的时候没有考上研究生，这便成了我的一个心结。在随后的工作中，"考研"如影随行，更是成为我追求的梦想。终于在我工作15年后，再次参加了全国硕士研究生统一考试，被新疆大学资源与环境科学学院录取，并在职硕博连读6年。此后，通过我的博士生导师及相关专家推荐，我有幸进入北京师范大学环境学院博士后流动站，与合作导师共同从事环境科学研究，两年后我顺利出站。

每个人都有过这样或那样的梦想，我认为人的一生应该至少有一次努力地追逐自己梦想的经历。每个人都有一个属于自己的甜美的梦，趁我们还年轻，努力去奋斗一次吧。

人，因有梦想而不平庸。我们无法决定自己的一切，但是我们的梦想是无价的。有了物质，那是生存；有了精神，那才是生活。人的一生唯有伟大的梦想会支撑我们走向成功！

请大家抽出一点时间来重新审视自己的生活吧，这本书就是大家审视自我的第一步。你的生活你做主——大家可以随自己的意愿改变自我，也可以选择安于现状、知足常乐。不管大家如何选择，我都衷心希望书中真实的故事能让你开拓思维，能让你获得快乐，也能让你感动落泪。我在完成书稿后，心中感触良多，希望书中的内容在给广大读者带来喜悦的同时，也能触动大家的心灵。

Once upon a while, I no longer think about my life, and just want to spend the rest of my life in a normal way. Comfort is my pursuit. Perhaps, everyone´s life is different because of different experiences and lifestyles. Although our lives are different, we can have our own choices. Everyone experiences success and failure, pleasure and pain, ordinary and frustrations in one´s lifetime. Because of this experience, our lives are not mediocre.

Everyone experiences many unforgettable things in his life. Because of setbacks, we learn to grow and overcome difficulties. If we have only happy in life, we will lack the ability to overcome pain. So how else can we feel happy? Life endow with us many difficulties, we grow up, mature and experience happiness among them.

Life is too short to waste. I was born in the late 1960s, my childhood was carefree until I was 6, followed by 15 years of schooling. Not having received the offer for the postgraduate school during my senior year was my biggest regret and it had even become a knot in my heart. In the days that followed, the dream of continuing postgraduate study accompanied me all the time. After 15 years´ of working, I took the national master´s examination again and I was admitted by the College of Resources and Environmental Sciences of Xinjiang University. With the recommendation of my tutor and related experts, I had the honor to enter the Post-doctoral Mobile Station of School of Environment of Beijing Normal University, and worked with my co-tutor in the environmental science research.Finally, I successfully completed the study two years later.

Everyone has various dreams. I think people should strive to pursue his own dreams at least once in his life. What kind life do you want to live? Everyone has a sweet dream belongs to his own, so why not struggle once while you are young?

A person is not mediocre because of his own dreams. We can't decide everthing about ourselves, but our dreams are priceless. It's the matter that affords people to surviue,but is the dream that makes people live.Only a great dream can support us to succeed!

This book is the first step in setting aside some time to take a look at your life. You are in charge of your life. You can make any changes that you want, or you can resolve to be satisfied and happy with what you already have. Whichever is the case, I sincerely hope that the real story in the book will make you think, laugh, and even cry. After writing the manuscript, I thought a lot, and hoped that the contents of the book would bring joy to the readers and touch everyone's soul too.

目 录

Contents

目

录

Contents

目　录

Contents

第 1 章　简单的快乐

Chapter 1　Simple Pleasures

一个人快乐与否不是由他所处的环境决定，而是他的心态。

A happy person is not a person in a certain set of circumstances, but rather a person with a certain set of attitudes.

* 烈士的后代
The Descendants of the Martyrs

　　20世纪60年代末的一个冬天，我出生在一个普通的兵团战士之家。那时我的外公刚去世五天。我的外公是一名军人，曾经担任过骑兵连指导员，复员后在兵团搞思想政治工作，去世后被追认为革命烈士。外婆是随军家属，外公去世后她一直领着抚恤金过日子，孤独终老。

　　我的家庭关系很简单，母亲出生在新疆巴里坤，是家里的独生女，那个年代确实是一个例外。父亲家里四个兄弟，父亲排行第三。我的奶奶最喜欢我父亲，因为我的父亲有文化，长得英俊，性格也好。物以稀为贵，奶奶没有女儿，就想要孙女，所以我一出生，她就专门从河南老家千里迢迢赶来新疆照看我，把我带到两三岁，后来，因为身体不好才回

父母在开封
My Father and Mother in Kaifeng

了河南老家。

我们家里有四个孩子，我排行第三。在我五岁的时候，我与母亲、大哥和弟弟回过一次老家——河南兰考县。我的父亲和二哥留下看家。因为兰考县没有什么亲戚了，就在开封市二伯家住了一段时间。那时记忆犹新的一件事就是我很调皮，直接用嘴对着水龙头喝自来水，被二伯拍了一下脑袋，说生水不能喝，然后我就大哭起来，认为二伯打我了。现在想想觉得自己那时真是娇气任性。

长大后，我和两个哥哥继承了外公和母亲的优良传统，积极要求进步，都先后加入了中国共产党，尤其是两个哥哥在各自的领导岗位上为国家和社会做出了重要的贡献。

One winter in the late 1960s, five days after my grandfather passed away, I was born in an ordinary home of the 7th Division Corps. My grandfather was a soldier. He served as an instructor for cavalry companies before. After demobilization, he engaged in ideological and political work in the Corps and was recognized as a revolutionary martyr after his death. My grandmother was an army dependent. After my grandfather died, she had been living with a pension and died alone.

My family relations are simple. My mother was born in Barkol of Xinjiang, and she was the only child in the family. It was indeed an exception in that era. My father has three other brothers and my father ranked third. My grandmother liked my father best because my father was educated, handsome and good -natured. The rare things are expensive. My grandmother had no daughter, so she expected a granddaughter. So as soon as I was born, she came all the way from her hometown in Henan to look after me in Xinjiang. She brought up me to two or three years old and returned to her hometown in Henan because of poor health.

We have four children in our family and I am the third. When I was 5 years old, with my mother, big brother and younger brother, I returned to my hometown -LanKao County in Henan. Because we had no relatives in LanKao County, we lived in uncle´s house in Kaifeng city for a period of time. My father and second brother stayed at home. The only thing I still remember for that period of time is that I was very naughty. I drank water directly from waterpipe and my uncle tapped me on my head. He said that raw water could not be drunk directly. Then I cried and thought that the uncle hit me. Now I feel that I was petulant at that time.

After growing up, my two elder brothers and I continued the good traditions of grandfather and mother, and actively demanded progress. We all successively joined the Communist Party of China. In particular, the two elder brothers have made great contributions to the society in their respective leadership.

* 母亲的快乐

Mother's Happiness

　　我是家里的独女，待遇和哥哥、弟弟不一样，至少每年都有新衣服穿。小时候，我穿的衣服都很鲜艳，花棉袄、花棉裤，简直就是一个"花姑娘"。那时我家还住在五连，家里基本上都是挑水做饭，我不需要干家务活，还觉得做家务都是男孩子的事情，比如说挑水、砍柴、生火等，做饭还是父母做得多些。

　　家里没柴火用了，就盼着刮大风，风停了之后，我们就可以排成一队，挎上篮子，一起出去捡柴火了。家里总是堆着很多木材。没事的时候，我们经常出去捡树枝，整整齐齐地堆在家里的院子前面；还出去上树摘沙枣。这些情景现在想起来觉得很温馨！

　　我唯一的弟弟，小时候长得白白胖胖的，很可爱。有一次弟弟调

院子里的树枝
Branches in the Yard

皮，干了错事不承认，母亲就想用小棍打他。其实是吓唬他，不舍得真打他。可是他吓得拔腿就跑，母亲追不上他，就大声说："你们给我把他抓回来。"我们从小可听话了，母亲是学校教师，对我们的教育很严格。我们一听到母亲的命令，立刻全部出动去追弟弟。当时弟弟穿的是一个平角短裤，小屁股胖乎乎的，跑起来一扭一扭的，而且换腿的频率很高，看着真好玩。他跑得快，我们都没有追上。他躲到牛圈里，我们抓不到他。后来，经过大家哄骗，才回了家。母亲没有打他，只是狠狠教训了他。类似的小插曲太多了，但这个情景记得很清楚，因为当时母亲也觉得好笑。母亲生前说起这件事时，总是笑个不停。母亲的笑容永远地留在了我的记忆里，我觉得母亲的快乐就是我们的快乐！

I am the only girl in the family. Unlike my elder brothers and one younger brother, I had new clothes every year. As a child, my clothes were all in very bright color, jacket and trousers with flower patterns, which made me look like a "flower girl". At that time, our family was still living in the 5th company, and almost every family needed to fetch water to cook, but I had no need to do housework. I felt that it was boy's work to fetch water, chop firewood, make a fire, and so on. Cooking was more often done by parents.

When there was no firewood in the house, we waited for the wind to blow. After the wind had stopped, we carried baskets and lined up, and went out to collect firewood. The house was always piled with a lot of firewood. When there was nothing happened, we often went out to pick up branches, piled neatly in front of the yard, and went out to pick angustifolia on trees. It's so sweet to recall all!

My only younger brother in his childhood was plump and cute. Once he did something wrong and didn't admit, my mother would beat him with a stick. In fact, my mother just wanted to scare him, and was not willing to really beat him. But he was so frightened then he ran away. My mother could not catch him, and she cried out, "Kids, get him back for me." We had been obedient all the time, my mother was school teacher and strict in our education. As soon as we heard our mother's order, we all went out to chase our younger brother. At that time, younger brother wore a pair of shorts. His little chubby butt wiggled forward with frequent legs alternation. He looked really funny and ran fast. We could not catch him because he hid in a cowshed. After everyone coaxed him, we got home together. My mother didn't beat him and just taught him a good lesson. There were so many similar episodes, and the scene was very clear, because my mother was amused at that time. When I was talking about this thing, mother always laughed. These smiles remain in my memory. I think our mother's happiness is our happiness!

* "面瘫"的经历
The Experience of "Face Paralysis"

从小没有人敢欺负我，都知道我有两个哥哥。上小学时，我非常要强，每次考试，语文和数学都要拿一百，要得第一名。记得有一次，我差两分没有拿到双百，就十分不高兴，站在院子里迎着风哭了很久。

晚上吃饭时，父亲说我的嘴怎么歪了，母亲走近一看，果然有点歪，立刻带着我去找王医生——我们连队唯一会针灸的医生。他给我一连扎了三天针，就基本上好了。刚开始扎针时没什么感觉，快好时就觉得疼了，哇哇直哭。王医生说幸好发现及时，加上我的年龄又小，恢复起来比较快。

一直以来，我对母亲充满感恩，只是没有直接说给母亲听而已。如果当时母亲没有带着我及时治疗，后果不堪设想。而今想到母亲的爱，我的眼泪不由自主地流了下来，后悔在母亲生前没有表达出

第七师 127 团五连
The 5th Company in the 127 Regiment
of the 7th Division

来。在我刚上初三时，父亲被调回团部大商店工作，我们举家迁到团部居住。

父亲脾气好，经常帮助别人，人缘很好，是单位上有名的老实人。有一天晚上，他在团部的商店替人值班，忘了关窗户，吹了风，嘴巴歪了。他赶紧去找王医生扎针，可因父亲年龄大了，最终没有完全复位，眼角有点斜。从此以后，只要外面有风，我就不敢说笑，嘴巴闭得紧紧的，真是"一朝被蛇咬，十年怕井绳"。

No one dared to bully me in my childhood because of my two older brothers. I was very competitive in elementary school. I had to take a hundred for every exam of Chinese and Mathematics. I rememberd one time, I did not get a double hundred because of two points missing, I was not happy, stood in the yard and cried for a long time.

At dinner, my father said my mouth seemed crooked, my mother checked and there as really a bit crooked, immediately they took me to Dr. Wang, the only doctor in the company who could acupuncture. After a three -day needle treatment, I was basically well. I did not feel the needle in the beginning, and felt the pain right before it would finish, then I began to cry loudly. Dr. Wang said it was good we went to him in time, and I was young which was good to recover quickly.

I have always been grateful to my mother! The consequences were unimaginable if my mother did not take me in time for the treatment. Thinking of mother's love, my tears involuntarily flow down. I regret not expressing my love to her when she was alive. When I just went to Grade Three of the junior high school, my father was transferred back to work at the regimental store and our family moved to the regimental headquarters.

My father is very popular and is a well-known honest person in the unit because of his good temper and helpful nature. One night, my father filled in for someone else at the regimental store and forgot to close the window. His mouth crooked due to the wind came in. He went to see Dr. Wang immediately. He eventually did not completely recover because of his age. The corner of his eye was a bit oblique, but not very obvious. Since then, as long as wind blows outside, I dare not talk and always shut my mouth. It's been "Once bitten, twice shy".

* 小时候的"糗事"

The "Embarrassment" in My Childhood

新疆哈密市是我长大后离家去得最远的地方。记得第一次坐火车去哈密时，我惊讶地说："火车怎么这么长啊！"把母亲都逗乐了，笑我是个傻孩子。哈密位于新疆东部，夏天特别热，气候比较干燥。每天

骡子 The Mule

中午的时候，人们一般不出门。那时哈密市的旱厕较多，可能是为了方便游客。

一天下午，我出门倒垃圾时，看见一头"大毛驴"站在厕所旁边。我很奇怪，回去就告诉母亲我所见，还给母亲边说边

20世纪80年代的绿皮火车
The Green Train in the 1980s

比画。母亲一听就笑了，告诉我那是骡子，是毛驴和马的后代，还说我是个"书呆子"，我有点不好意思地笑了。

我上小学时，

有一次，母亲让我去买醋，我边走边念叨醋，害怕忘了买什么，可一不小心被门槛绊了一下，转身就给说成酱油了。后来母亲把这件事说得有板有眼的，把亲戚们都逗乐了。

Hami City in Xinjiang is the farthest place I went since I grew up. It was the first time I took a train, I was surprised and said, "Why is the train so long?" My mother was amused and called me silly girl! Hami is located in the eastern part of Xinjiang, it is very hot and dry in summer. People usually don´t go out at noon every day. At that time, there were many pit toilets in Hami, which may be for the convenience of tourists.

One afternoon, when I went to throw the garbage, I happened to see a "big donkey" standing next to a pit toilet. I was surprised and went back to tell my mother what I had seen. She smiled and told me that it was a mule, the descendant of donkey and horse. She said I was a "nerd". I smiled a little embarrassed.

When I was in elementary school, she once asked me to buy vinegar. I walked and murmured vinegar. I was afraid of forgetting what to buy. But I accidentally stumbled over the threshold and bought soy sauce right after I got up. Later, mother told the story vividly, and made the relatives laugh.

*轻松学习

Enjoy Studying

　　我是在母亲的唠叨下长大的，从小她就对我严加管教和呵护有加。那时兵团的水质不好，含氟较高，很多人都有氟斑牙，一些老年人还得了关节病。母亲敦促我从小养成晨跑的好习惯，我一直坚持到大三。我们兄妹四个在那个年代都很少生病，可谓母亲的智慧之处。因为她从小身体就不好，"久病成医"不是没有道理的。

　　家里里里外外的大小事情都是母亲操心，父亲是家里的配角，人们常说的"一物降一物"大概就是这个意思。母亲的愿望是上大学，可惜由于身体的原因，错过了考试，错过了就是一辈子。

　　我的学习很轻松。通常在课间休息时就能完成作业，感觉学习很有趣、轻松和快乐，尤其是在整个年级的考试

第七师 127 团五连学校
The 5th Company School in the 127 Regiment
of the 7th Division

中，只有我一个人能解决难题，那种满足感和成就感难以形容。那时很多同学羡慕我，我全然不知，只陶醉在快乐里。成年后的同学聚会才得知这些信息。

我成了母亲的理想实现者，同时也继承了母亲的优点——记性好。每天晚上睡觉前，我躺在床上，再现当天上课的情景，温故而知新。在母亲的督促和关爱下，中学期间，我的学习成绩一直名列前茅，三年初中和两年高中都是学习委员和"三好学生"，高考前我被评为地区级"三好学生"，高考成绩加 10 分，母亲很是欣慰！

I grew up under the nagging of my mother, and she had taught and cared for me since I was a child. At that time, the water quality of the Corps was not good, in which the fluorine content was high, and the dental flurosis were common. Many elderly people had joint disease. My mother urged me to develop the good habit of jogging in the morning since I was a child. We all were rarely ill at that time owe to the wisdom of our mother. She was in poor health. It was reasonable to "become a doctor after long illness".

My mother took care of everything in and out of the house. And it made my father less important in the family. It is said that one thing can conquer another one. That was what happened between my mother and father. My mother wished to go to college. Unfortunately, she did not catch the exam for her poor health condition and missed it for a lifetime.

Study was an easy thing for me then. I usually finished my homework at school. Study was interesting, relaxed and happy for me. Especially in the exam for the whole grade, I was the only one who could answer the difficult questions. That sense of satisfaction and accomplishment was indescribable! At that time, many students envied me. I did not realize it at all and was only intoxicated with happiness. I got to know it in a class reunion many years later.

I became the ideal implementer of my mother and inherited her good memory. Every night, I recalled what teachers taught during the day right before I went to sleep. To review the old so as to learn the new. Under the supervision and care of my mother, I had always maintained my academic performance in the top in the middle school. Among the three years of junior high school and two years of senior high school, I was the commissary in charge of studies and a "Merit Student" all the time. Before the college entrance examination, I was rated as "Merit Student" at the regional level which brought me ten extra scores in the college entrance exam. Mother was very happy!

* "四人组合"的感悟

The Understanding of Group-of-Four

那时的孩子一般都是七岁才上学，可我五岁时想上学，因为年龄太小，就当起了旁听生。不知不觉中上完了小学。我的长相也完成了从"丑小鸭"到"黑牡丹"的蜕变，其实就是人们常说的"长开了"。

上初中时，班里有三个从小一起长大的男生，都是班干部。我是班里的学习委员，偶然组成了一个类似"四人组合"的小团队。我们彼此合作，使我们班的所有工作都发挥得淋漓尽致。这就是现在所谓的"团队精神"吧。我的工作主要是收作业，帮助差生及时完成当天的作业，抱着全班的作业本送到任课老师家，经常很晚才回家，我是老师的得力助手。每年的"三好学生"都有我，我当之无愧！

我跟随父母来到团部学校上初三，班里的男女同学之间基本上不交流，班主任抓得紧，都忙着中考；高中两年，大家又都忙着学习，准备考大学，母亲对我很严厉，我也就顾不上搞"四人组合"。上大学时，我继续担任学习委员，还结交了三个爱好比较接近的"铁哥们"。延续中学的传统，我们还叫"四人组合"，现在叫"朋友圈"，不同的是，我们经常在一起学习和玩耍。

在大学，只要你学得好，就会有人找你帮助。除了上课外，我们"四人组合"经常进行棋类活动，我喜欢上了下围棋。进行野外考察时我们分在一个组，互帮互助，享受着团队生活带来的快乐和开心，四年的大学生活也过得很惬意！

At that time, children were usually seven years old when they could go to school. When I was five years old, I wanted to go to school, and became an auditor. I unwittingly completed primary school, and my appearance also completed the transformation from an ugly duckling into a black peony. That was what people often called "Face Grow".

In junior high school, there were three boys who grew up together with me and were all class cadres. I was commissary in charge of studies in the class. We accidentally formed a small team "Group-of-Four" and collaborated with each other to make the best of all the work in our class. This is what is now called "team spirit". Of course, my responsibility was mainly to collect homework and helped the poor students to complete their homework of the day in time. I often got home very late, and carried assignments to the teacher's home, and I was the teacher's right-hand assistant and the so-called "little teacher". "Merit Student" in every year had my name. I deserved it!

When I was in the Third Grade of junior high school, We moved and I transferred to the regimental school. Boys and girls at new school did not communicate with each other often. Teachers managed them strictly only for the purpose of high school entrance exam. During the two years in high school, we were busy studying and preparing for the university. My mother was very strict with me, so I could not spare time for Group-of-Four. After I went to college, I continued to serve as commissary in charge of studies. I also made three iron buddies. Our hobbies were relatively similar. Continuing the tradition of high school, we also called Group-of-Four and now called the circle of friends. The difference is that we often meet and communicate.

In college, as long as you learn well, someone will come to you for help. In addition to having class, our Group-of-Four often played chess, and I like to play Weiqi too. In the field practice class, we were grouped together. We helped each other and enjoyed the happiness of the team life, four-year college life was also very pleasant!

* 更简单的快乐

Simpler Pleasures

上高中时，家里的生活条件有所改善，有了自来水和鼓风机。母亲什么家务活都不让我做，希望我好好学习，将来考上一所好大学。一方面，上大学我可以离开兵团，不用种地；另一方面，上大学也是她的理想，这是一种心理补偿。父母都很宠我，夏天的西瓜，如果是沙瓢子，我就先吃西瓜心；吃晚饭时，所有的菜汤先倒进我的米饭碗里。

记得二哥曾经打过我一次，他现在竟然不承认，他可能忘了，可我还记得清楚。当时不知是否是自己的错，反正就是一直不理他，心里嘀咕父母都没有打过我，你竟敢打我，真是敢冒"天下之大不韪"。后来他跟我道歉，我快乐地接受了。

现在每年过年，全家聚在一起，只要有人提起小时候的事，基本上都是异口同声地"声讨"我：小时候家务活干的最少、好东西吃的最多，等等。我觉得那时候好像也没有什么好吃的东西。上高中时，每年过生日，我唯一的愿望就是吃江米条。父亲从商店给我拿回来新鲜的江米条，我就很高兴，非常满足。那时候快乐就是这么简单！

Our life got much better when I was in high school, we could use tap water and blowers. My mother did not let me do housework. My mother hoped me to study hard and go to college. On the one hand, I could leave the life of working in the Corps; on the other hand, going to the university was her dream, which was a psychological compensation. My parents spoiled me in the family. The best part of a watermelon was for me and the best vegetable soup was poured into my bowl.

I remember my second brother once slapped me, and now he does not admit. He may forget, I still remember it clearly. I didn't know whether it was my fault, but just kept ignoring him. I told myself our parents had never hit me. How dare you do it? Later, when he apologized, I forgave him happily.

Every New Year, the whole family can get together. As long as anyone recalled our childhood, basically everyone began to "condemning" me for doing the least housework and eating the best food. There were not much delicious snacks in our life then. My only wish on each birthday in high school was to eat a snack called rice bar. My father brought me fresh rice bars from the store, and I was very happy and satisfied. Happiness was so simple then!

* 意外的遇见

Unexpected Encounter

　　大学生活的最后一个夏天，让人很眷恋。我的一个好朋友，在新疆大学锅炉房上班，经人介绍，要与一个男同志见面，他是新疆大学保卫科的科员，乌鲁木齐市人。那个时候有乌鲁木齐户籍的人很受欢迎。那时候的人们思想比较保守，她不好意思单独见面，让我陪她一起去，我不假思索地就同意了。任何人的遇见都是缘分，也就是这场相亲，开启了我的另一段人生之旅。

　　"五一"的时候，他们相约在人民公园见面。有趣的是，这个科员也带了一个好友。估计是面子薄，也想让好友给参谋一下。这个科员和他的好友都是四川人，好友是新疆大学生物系大三的学生。自我介绍后，大家都认识了。

　　这个科员长得还不错，浓眉大眼，身高中等，与我的好朋友还是蛮般配的。我还是第一次去人民公园。五月的公园，有些花已经开了，景色还不错。好朋友比较喜欢那个科员，后来两个人开始约会，我开始忙于自己的毕业事宜。

　　多年之后的一天，我在街上偶遇了这个朋友，才知道他们因为我好朋友的户籍迁不进乌鲁木齐市而分开了。而我和那个生物系男生，却因为他们的约会而相识，直至走入婚姻殿堂。前几天，我还和老公去了人民公园，故地重游，唤起我们相识时的回忆，毕竟过去 30 年了，物是人非。

乌鲁木齐人民公园（2018）
The People's Park in Urumqi(2018)

巧合的是，我们还是"五一"领的结婚证，看来都是命运的安排！应验了一个商校女生的预言，她曾经说我将来的结婚对象来自遥远的地方。我当时还犟，说我如果找身边的人结婚呢，她说那这事肯定成不了。四川离新疆确实很遥远。

千里姻缘一线牵，这就是人们常说的缘分吧！从某种意义上来说，世间一切都是遇见，就像冷遇见暖，就有了雨；春遇见冬，就有了岁月；天遇见地，就有了永恒。

The last summer of college life was enchanting. Through a matchmaker's introduction, a good friend of mine, who worked in the boiler room of Xinjiang University, met with a young man, who was a security guard of Xinjiang University and had his ID in Urumqi which was very popular at that time. People were still conservative then. She felt embarrassed to meet the young man alone and asked me to accompany her and I agreed with no hesitation. Anyone's encounter is predestined. It is the blind date that opened another journey of my life.

On May 1st, the International Labor Day, they had an appointment in the People's Park. Interestingly, the young man went there with one of his friends. He was shy and wanted his friend to give him suggestion. They were both from Sichuan. His friend was a junior student in the Department of Biology of Xinjiang University. After self-introduction, we all knew each other.

The young man was a good-looking man with big eyes, medium height, and they well matched with each other. It was the first time that I went to the People's Park. In May, some of the flowers were already in bloom and the view was quite good in the park. My friend liked that young man. Then, they began to date each other regularly. But I was busy with my graduation during that time.

One day after many years, I met this friend in the street and knew that they had broken up because my friend failed to transfer her ID to Urumqi. Instead, the young man's friend from the Department of Biology and I got in touch and got married finally after their dating. A few days ago, my husband and I visited the People's Park again to recall our memories in 1980s. Thirty years had passed, which brought change to nothing but us.

What a coincidence, we registered our marriage on the International Labor Day. It seems like the arrangement of the fate! A girl from business school read my palm one time and said my husband would be from a distant place. I was stubborn and did not believe it. I wanted to marry a man from our area. She said I would not succeed to do so. Finally, her words came true. Sichuan is indeed more than two thousand kilometers away from Xinjiang.

Fate brings people who are far apart together. In a sense, everything in the world is for meeting one another. There is rain when the cold meets the warm. There is year when spring meets winter. There is eternity when heaven meets earth.

* 小插曲

A Brief Interlude

很快就要离开学校了，我的工作还没有找到，在乌鲁木齐又没有什么亲戚，因此有些心灰意冷。离开兵团就不想再回去，准备慢慢找工作。有一天，我站在宿舍楼门口的大树下，等同学搬行李出来。忽然听到有人叫我，回头一看，好像不认识，他说："你不认识我了吗？'五一'在人民公园见过的。"

"哦，对。"我开始有点不好意思了，想起是那个生物系的男生。他了解情况后，一拍胸脯说："我保证帮你找到工作，暑假我陪你找工作。"我已经走投无路，只有碰碰运气！

我们联系了大哥的大学同学，然后找到了他父母的家——昌吉试验场。我后来就在那里

新疆大学女生宿舍楼门口
The Doorway in the Girls' Dormitory
of Xinjiang University

的学校工作了。那里有点像一个农村的缩影，到处是农田，是个试验基地。学校里学生很少，都是试验场职工的后代。从一年级到初三，都是单班，一个班也就20个人左右，有的年级人更少。冬天教室里要用柴火和煤生火取暖，就是在那个时候我学会了生炉子。

试验场办公场所不大，门口有条宽敞的马路，看上去与我的兵团之家差不多。

新疆水利厅昌吉试验场（2018）
The Changji Experimental Field of the Water Conservancy Department in Xinjiang (2018)

以前二哥曾经来过这里，现在有时还念叨这个地方，说想不到一个大学毕业生，工作环境还不如兵团。以前我学的专业比较好分配工作，后来毕业的大学生，必须回原来的居住地工作，甚至需要下基层锻炼三到五年。可想而知，我的第一个工作单位条件虽然差些，但能留下来工作已算很幸运。

说起来我能留在试验场学校工作，是凭我自己的实力留下来的。我的英语课试讲成功，并且顺利通过场领导面试。这其中还有个小插曲。有一天，遇见场长，他说我长得像他的初恋女友。他的年龄都是我的长辈了，我以为他是开玩笑。记得当时他还对我说："你年轻，又有男朋友了，好日子还长着呢，好好工作吧！"场长是个转业军人，待人正直、宽容。时过境迁，我渐渐地理解了那个年代人们的生活。

I would soon leave college, and my job was nowhere to find. I had no relatives in Urumqi. I was disheartened. I did not want to go back to the Corps and decided to do my job hunting patiently. One day, I stood under the big tree in front of the dormitory building, waiting for my classmates to move the luggage out. Suddenly I heard someone calling me, looking back confused and he said, "Don't you remember me? We met in the People's Park on May 1st. ""Oh, yes. " I felt embarrassed. It's the young man from the Department of Biology. He asked me about my situation and promised to accompany and help me find a job in summer vacation. I had no choice and had to try my luck!

We contacted my old brother's college classmate, and then found his parents' home——Changji Experimental Field, I worked in school there later. It was a rural microcosm. It was full of farmland and was a testing base. There were not too many students in the school and they were the kids of workers in the Experimental Field. There was only one class in each grade from Grade One to Grade Nine. There were only about or less than 20 students in each grade. It was at that time that I learned how to make a fire with firewood and coal in the classroom in winter.

The office space at the Experimental Field was small. There

was a wide road in front of the doorway. It looked very much like my home at Corp's. My second brother visited me once and he still recalled this place sometimes. He said that he didn't expect the working environment of a college graduate was not so good as that in the Corps. At that time, my major had more advantages in distributing work. Later, everyone must return to work in their original place of residence and even need to exercise at the grassroots level for three to five years. As it can be imagined, I was lucky enough to work there, even though my first job was in poor condition.

By the way, I was able to stay and work in the school due to my own advantage. The demo English class I gave was successful, and I successfully passed the interview of leadership in the Experimental Field. There's a little episode here. One day, when the director met me alone, he said I looked like his first girlfriend. He's old enough to be my elder, so I thought that was a joke. I remember he told me, "You are young and have a boyfriend, you have a bright future. Just work on it. " The director was an ex-serviceman with Xinjiang person's forthrightness and tolerance. As time passed by, I gradually understand the people's personal life in that era.

* 营养炖
Nutritious Stew

　　新疆大学生物系的这个男生，虽然在大学比我低一届，但是比我大两岁，而且很有经济头脑。生物系上课要用青蛙做实验，他自告奋勇地承担了货源的任务。因为他知道我们试验场青蛙多，由大哥同学的父母带头，收购了青蛙，然后交给学校。他和新疆长大的男生不一样，人很幽默，时常让我很开心。

　　每次周末或节假日，他基本上都来试验场看我。从公交车

站到试验场没有公交车，要走三公里石子铺的路。他总是买水果，从来不买鲜花，说新疆干燥，要多补充水分，买鲜花是乱花钱，不值得！我没有异议，只是笑笑，这就养成爱吃水果的习惯了。

　　那个时候，大学毕业生要求无偿献血，只要满足条件就要献血。女生体

通往昌吉试验场的路
The Road to Changji Experimental Field

重 45 公斤以下不用献血，我毕业时体重是 44 公斤没有献血。而他符合条件就献了血。我在试验场给他买了一只老母鸡，送到新疆大学生物系实验室。我们用实验室高压锅做鸡汤，放了些调料，给他补身体。夏天温度高，气味大，被值班老师闻到了。听到有老师的脚步声过来，我们赶紧盖好盖子，把门关紧，躲了起来。两个老师走过去了，边走还边说，哪来的鸡肉香味，我们俩偷偷地笑了。那时候的日子真的很开心，我至今还很怀念。

The boy in the Department of Biology of Xinjiang University is two years older than me, though he was one-level below me in the college, and he really had an economic mind. The Department of Biology needed frogs in their experiments. He volunteered for the task of frog supply because he knew there were a lot of frogs at the Experimental Field. Parents of my brother's college classmate took the lead in buying frogs. Then he sold to their department. Unlike the boys who grew up in Xinjiang, he was humorous and often made me happy.

On every weekend or holiday, he walked three kilometers of unpaved road to see me because there was no bus from the station to the Experimental Field. He always bought fruit for me, but never bought flowers. He said Xinjiang was dry and fruit had plenty of nutrition and water that our body needed, buying flowers was a waste of money. I did not refute and just smiled every time when he did so. He developed my habit of eating fruits.

At that time, you should donate blood as long as you met the physical requirement. Girls did not need to donate blood for weighing below 45 kilograms. I was only 44 kilograms then. And he met the boy's condition and donated blood. I bought him an old hen at the Experimental Field and sent it to the Laboratory of the Department of Biology of Xinjiang University. We made chicken soup with the lab pressure cooker to build up his health. In summer, the temperature was high, so the soup had a strong smell. The teacher on duty smelled it. Hearing the teacher's footsteps, we quickly put on the lid and closed the door, and then hid. The two teachers went past the lab and said, "Where does the smell of chicken come from?" We both laughed quietly. At that time, we were really very happy. I still cherish it so far.

第 2 章 从此刻开始

Chapter 2　From This Moment On

有些梦想看起来遥不可及，一旦我们下定决心，这些梦想就触手可及。

　　So many of our dreams seem improbable, and then, when we summon the will, they soon became inevitable.

*人生的改变
The Change of Life

　　中学时，"四人组合"中的班长，是和我从小一起长大的"发小"，一直被我们称为"书呆子"。理论上讲，比我还"呆"，我是考虑问题"呆"，他是连说话都"呆"。他的一大特点就是考试时有把握的题才做，保证得分，否则就不做。偶尔，他的见解会不一般，尤其是他认准的事，打死不回头，是个不见棺材不落泪的主！但是他做事很细心，并且有分寸，不愧是我们的"老班长"。

　　都说性格决定命运，我的经历得到了验证。高考前某一天，班主任老师找我谈话，说我一定可以考上大学，让我把高考可以加的10

第七师 127 团团部中学（2008）
The Regimental Middle School in the 127 Regiment
of the 7th Division(2008)

分，让给这个"老班长"。我知道"老班长"家里确实困难，姊妹还多，他的父母与我的父母都认识。他的父母身体都不好，母亲工作时，不小心被机器"吃"了一只手，变成了残疾人。以我当时的成绩考上大学是板上钉钉的事，我的个性和傲气决定了我不假思索地就同意了，而且还忘了告诉母亲。

等到母亲知道这个事情的时候，已经无法挽回。我受到了母亲有史以来最严厉的批评。后来由于高考成绩加10分的谦让，本应上重点院校——北京医学院的我，却因高考成绩差6分，阴差阳错地被参考志愿里的新疆大学录取了。当时年少轻狂的我没有丝毫后悔，多年之后，才逐渐明白自己的人生轨迹就此改变了。

In high school, the monitor, one of Group-of-four, was my best friend and we grew up together. He was called book dumb all the time. Theoretically, he was stiffer than me. I looked stiff when I was thinking, but he was stiff even when he was talking. He had a habit that he only did the questions in exams that he was sure to be right, otherwise he would rather leave the exam paper blank. For a few times, he would have different opinions, especially on the things he insisted. No one could convince him to change his mind. At the same time, he was careful and tactful in dealing with issues of our class. He proved himself to be a good monitor.

It is said personality is your destiny. I verified it with my experience. One day before the College Entrance Exam, my class advisor came and talked to me, he wanted me to give up my 10 extra scores I earned and give it to the monitor because he was sure I could pass the Exam definitely. I knew the monitor was from a poor family and he had several siblings. His parents and my parents also knew each other well. And his parents were not in good health condition, especially his mother, who lost one hand in a machine when she was working. According to my normal academic performance, I was sure I could pass the Exam and go to college, so I agreed immediately without discussing with my mother.

It was too late to do anything when my mother knew it. My mother gave me a harshest criticism in my life. Unfortunately, I was 6 scores less after the Exam, so I missed the chance to go to Beijing Medical College, instead, I had to go to Xinjiang University. I did not regret at all to give up my extra 10 scores at that time. But as time passed by, I realized my life was completely changed from then.

*晨跑者的自白
Morning Runner's Confessions

　　新疆大学地理系 1985 年招收了两个班——水文班和地理班。水文班是隔年招生，一年招汉族班，一年招维吾尔族班；招生的人数都不多，而且招的都是理科生。当年水文班招收了 20 个理科生，其中女生 5 个，我们不住在同一个宿舍，与地理班女生混住。

　　我喜欢清静，大学四年，一直住上铺，拉上帘子就是自己的一个小天地。我继续坚持着中学时代的早睡早起、晨跑的习惯。室友们经常夜谈，我总是准时睡觉，而且睡觉很沉，她们

的"夜话"我一概不知。有一次住在我下铺的女生睡着了，点着的蜡烛把我的褥子烧了一半，味道很大，把她呛醒了，我都

新疆大学的女生宿舍楼
The Building of the Girls' Dormitory in Xinjiang University

不知道。

　　夏天的一个晚上，天气闷热，我们没有关窗户。那时我们住一楼，有防护栏，我住在靠窗的上铺。一天半夜睡得正香，感觉头顶有哗啦啦的声音。起初以为做梦，后来声音越来越大，我就被惊醒了，睁开眼往窗外一看，吓了一跳，看见有个黑影蹲在窗户下面，用一个铁钩子正在钩我挂在靠近窗户那头的小包，床头也是铁制的，碰到后在安静的夜里声音很大。我大喊一声："谁？"那人做贼心虚，听到我的喊叫，受惊吓后，丢下铁钩就跑了。事后室友都夸我胆大，其实，那晚是我生平第一次失眠。

Department of Geography in Xinjiang University enrolled two classes in 1985, one was Hydrology class and the other was Geography class. The Hydrology class enrolled Han students one year and enrolled Uygur students next year. It only enrolled several science students each year. In 1985, the Hydrology class enrolled twenty science students, including five female students. We did not live in the same dormitory. We lived together with girls in Geography class.

I liked to have privacy. I lived in the upper bed for four years. My curtain on the bed made me a small quiet place. I continued my habit of sleeping early, getting up early and going for a jogging every morning. My roommates always talked late in the night, but I went to sleep early so I never knew what they were talking about. The girl lived below me fell asleep one time and she forgot to blow out her candle. The candle burned part of my bedding with a bad burning smell which choked her and awakened her. However, I knew nothing about it.

One summer night, it was hot that we did not close the window. Our dormitory was on the first floor and there were fences on the window. My bed was by the window. I was soundly sleeping at midnight. Suddenly, I heard some noises over my head. I thought I was in a dream at first, but the noise got louder and louder, I was awakened. I was shocked when I looked out of the window. A shadow squatted outside of the window and was reaching for the purse hanging on my bed with a iron hook. The bed frame was made of steel, so it made a loud noise in the silent night. I shouted loudly, "Who is there?" The guilty conscience made the shadow scared in my shout, so he ran away with his hook left behind. My roommates praised me of my braveness. Actually, that night was my first sleepless night.

*坦然面对

Let's Face It

　　大哥的一个大学同学在乌鲁木齐工作，他的父母家在昌吉的一个试验场，这是新疆水利厅的一个直属单位。这个单位的学校缺少英语和地理老师，我都可以胜任，因为我从小就喜欢英语。我的母亲曾经当过小学数学老师，我知道母亲的辛苦，所以不愿意当老师。

新疆水利厅昌吉试验场池塘
The Pond of Changji Experimental Field of the Water Conservancy Department in Xinjiang

人在屋檐下，不得不低头。走一步看一步，是不是自己喜欢的工作已经不重要了，重要的是自己可以留在昌吉。我的报到证在水利厅，如果昌吉试验场学校同意接收我，开个接收证明，我就可以留下。我心里很期盼，觉得曙光就在眼前！

那个生物系的男生说到做到，每天都陪着我出去找工作。暑假期间，母亲一直关心我的工作。最后，我还是变成了一个教育工作者。长大后，我就成了你！歌词如现实。

三十年后的今天，我才渐渐明白，当初自己选择的不仅仅是一个职业，更重要的是自己为这个社会做了什么，自己的社会价值和人生价值如何体现出来！人应该对自己的选择负责任，只要问心无愧，坦然面对一切，时间会公正地回报每一个曾经付出过努力的人！

One of my eldest brother′s college classmates worked in U-rumqi, whose parents were in the Changji Experimental Field, which was a directly subordinate unit of the Water Conservancy Department in Xinjiang. The unit needed English teachers and Geography teachers badly, I could do both well because I loved English since I was little. My mother once was a math teacher in a primary school, so I knew how hard it was to be a teacher and I was not willing to do it.

People have to bow under the eaves. It was not important

whether I liked the job or not, and it was important whether I could stay in Changji. My report card was in Water Conservancy Department, and if the school of the Experimental Field could accept me then I could stay. I was looking forward to it and I felt the bright future was in the front.

The young man from the Department of Biology acted as he said, he went out with me every day and accompanied me when I was applying for jobs. My mother concerned a lot about my job during the summer vacation. Finally, I became a teacher. I turn into what you are when I grow up! The reality is going on just as the lyrics.

I begin to understand after thirty years, what I chose is not only a job, it has more significant meaning in what I have done in the society and how does my social value and the value of the life demonstrate. People should be responsible for his own choice. As long as he has a clear conscience, time will report back on what he has done fairly.

* 不忘初心

Remain True to Our Original Aspiration

　　工作一年后我调到了地质队子校工作。与那个生物系男生在一起教学，一年后成了家，一晃就是十年。这期间，家里就没有间断过亲戚。他家的亲戚比较多，主要来给我们帮忙。先是公婆，中间回过四川一次，两年后又回来带孙子。接着是老公的舅舅、大妹、二姐一家、外甥女等，先后来帮忙。老公工

新疆地矿局第一地质大队大门 (2017)
The Gate of the First Geology Team of the Bureau of
Geology and Mineral Resources in Xinjiang(2017)

作三年后就下了海，我一个人带着儿子，有点忙不过来。尤其是公婆回四川那段时间，我的母亲曾经过来与我住了半年。

时光如梭，但是我心里的那个梦想一直没有忘记，经常在学校领导开会的时候，坐在会议室靠窗一个不太引人注意的位置，手里拿着大学英语看着，心里想着要是能考上研究生就好了。英语是我的爱好之一，每天不看看它，就好像缺点什么似的，真是母亲曾说过的"书呆子"。

那时我的一个大学同学在吐鲁番水文局上班，他告诉我新疆大学正在招收在职研究生，不用入学考试，直接就读，利用节假日上课，毕业证好拿，只是学位证要通过英语和政治考试才可以拿到，每年学费三千多元。钱先暂且不说，就是不考试就可以入校读研究生，我就觉得不靠谱，况且我当时也没有那么多钱，觉得不正规，就谢绝了。但是，我仍然没有放弃温习英语。

One year later, I was transferred to the school of Geology Team. The young man from the Department of Biology was also a teacher there. We got married one year later. In the next ten years, relatives were coming and going all the time, especially relatives from his side to come and help us. My parents-in-law went back to Sichuan one time and came back two years later to help us take care of our child. Then his uncle, younger sister, elder sister´s family and his female nephew came and helped us from time to time. My husband quitted his job after three years of working and he started to do his business. I took care of our son by myself. It was too busy for me to handle. My mother even came and helped me for half a year when my parents-in-law went back to Sichuan.

Time flied by,but the dream was always in my mind. I always sat in the unnoticed corner in the conference room in school meeting and held a college English book in my hands. I thought how wonderful it would be if I could go for a master study. I love English. My life was like to lack something if I did not read English every day. I acted like a bookworm as my mother called me.

One of my college classmates was working in Turpan Hy-dropraphic Bureau at that time,he told me Xinjiang University was enrolling new on-the-job master students,without taking exams and classes were held on weekends and holidays. It was easy to got a graduation certificate,but the degree certificate could be got after you passed the English and Politics exams. The annual tuition was more than three thousand RMB. Despite the tuition,I felt it was not reliable because you could be a master student without passing an exam. And I also did not have enough money at the time,so I declined it with thanks. However,I still did not give up studying English.

* "蝎子"的启示
The Revelation of "Scorpion"

说起蝎子，现在还隐约心有余悸。我们去地质队工作之前，队里曾有人养过蝎子。有一段时间市场对蝎子的需求量大。后来不挣钱了，养蝎人就离开了地质队，留下了蝎子的后代，继续繁衍生息，结果给队上职工的身心带来了无穷无尽的折磨。蝎子跑得整个大队到处都是，被咬的人接二连三，医院也为此事忙起来了，私人诊所也红火起来了。我们来到地质队工作时，略有耳闻，没有当回事。

一天晚上睡觉时，蝎子从顶棚上掉到了床上，我们不知道。早上起床，一起身，估计碰到了蝎子，它就攻击了我，咬在腰上，真疼，幸好腰上有些肉，但也疼了好几天。老公喝酒，身上有酒味，没有咬到他。他立刻把床单挂在外面，找到蝎子后，拿钳子夹住，放在煤气灶上就烧成灰了。据说蝎子咬的第一口最厉害，后面的毒性逐渐

新疆地矿局地质一大队食堂
The Canteen of the First Geology Team of the
Bureau of Geology and Mineral Resources in Xinjiang

减弱。渐渐地我们也积累了一些经验，活蝎子夹住后泡酒，用此酒擦拭被咬之处可以缓解疼痛，但也只能暂时起作用。如果被蝎子咬在重要部位，有动脉血管的地方，还需要去医院或诊所打封闭针，以防毒液传到心脏，造成严重后果。

在地质队工作了十年，与蝎子斗争了五年。期间我被咬过两次，第二次是咬在手指上，五指连心，疼得无法入睡，把手指泡在醋里，效果也不明显。还有两个同事在同一天被蝎子咬，真是"有苦共享"。儿子四岁时，晚上被蝎子咬了一口，在后脑勺上。老公立即跑过去，抱住儿子的头，用嘴猛吸，吸一口往外吐一口，一会儿，儿子哭声就小了，然后再抹点"蝎子酒"。第二天，儿子就好多了，这是我们摸索出来的又一个相对有效的对付蝎子的办法。

人与自然和谐相处（梵蒂冈）
The Harmonious Coexistence between Human and Nature(Vatican)

"蝎子"一般不会主动进攻人类，当它觉得受到攻击或威胁时，才会毫不犹豫地咬你一口，而且毒性很大。蝎子毒的药效很好，可以被人类充分利用。所以爱护动物，和谐相处，扬长避短，未必不是一件好事！

I have not yet got over the scare as I mention the scorpion. Before we went to work in Geology Team, someone in the team raised scorpions because there was a large market demand once. Later, as the market demand dropped, people raised scorpions left the Geology Team, but he left the scorpion offsprings behind and they unfortunately multiplied in great quantity, which brought us endless nightmare. Scorpions ran over in the Geology Team everywhere, and more and more people were bitten. The hospital, even the private clinic, got busy for this. We heard about it when we got there but we did not pay attention.

One night, one scorpion fell onto the bed from the ceiling when we were asleep, and we did not know it. In the morning, it bit me on my waist when we got up. It was so hurt though I got thick flesh on my waist. My husband drank some wine before he went to sleep so the scorpion did not bite him. He hung the sheet out of our room, found the scorpion on the sheet, grabbed it with piers and burned it into ash on a gas cooker. It was said that the scorpion's first bite was most dangerous and then its poison got weaker. We gradually gathered some experience. We caught scorpions alive and put it in the wine. Wipping the bite with this wine would release the pain scorpion bit temporarily. If the scorpion bit on important parts of people, like arterial vessels, you need go to hospital immediately to get a shot to avoid the poison damaging heart.

We worked in the Geology Team for ten years and we fought against scorpions for five years. I was bitten twice during then. The second time it bit me on my finger. The fingers are linked to the heart. I was too hurt to go to sleep, so I soaked the finger into vinegar, but it did not work. Another two colleagues were bitten at the same day, we became fellow sufferers. When my son was four years old, he got a bite on the back of his head one night. My husband held him and sucked on his head immediately. He sucked and spat for several times, and my son stopped crying. We put some scorpion wine on his head, he was much better the second day. We found out another way to deal with scorpion bite.

Scorpion will not attack people actively. It will bite people only when it is attacked or threatened. Scorpion poison has good medical effect, and human can use it wisely. Loving the nature, living harmoniously with all creatures and adopting their good points are good in human development.

* 白手起家

Build Home from Nothing

　　虽然老公下了海，但我还是坚持工作，论资排辈，分到一套昌吉地质村的楼房。随后的寒暑假，我都带着儿子与老公住在昌吉地质村。现在这套房子还在，老公的大姐夫退休后，老两口从阿勒泰青河县来昌吉养老，在那儿住了四年。值得一提的是，老公当年到新疆投靠亲戚，考上新疆大学，就是他这个大姐夫的功劳，否则也没有我们的故事了，因此老公一直心存感激之情，把他们当作再生父母一样对待！

　　那时家里的钱老公都拿来炒股，基本上亏完了，他仅仅是投机行为，不会投资，最后只剩下几万元，我赶紧让他全部拿出来做生意。我在地质队工作的最后两年，我们在乌鲁木齐火车南站租了房子，这里交通便利，与一个四川老乡一起从事印章行业。为了尽快挣

四川成都的家外景（2017）

The Outdoor Scene of Our Home in Chengdu, Sichuan（2017）　**051**

钱，我们利用暑假去上海学习电脑刻章，代替手工刻章，省时省力，儿子就临时放在兵团的二哥家。

为了节约钱，我们在上海住的最便宜的房子，为了节约时间，我们分头培训学习，我学习电脑操作，他学习刻章机维修，一个星期就学会了。那时我们只有股市上拿出来的几万元钱，没有亲戚朋友可以借钱。我们在上海买了一台刻章机和一个电脑桌，加上来回的车票、住宿等费用，回来之后，可以说是一贫如洗了。但是我们有信心从头开始，因为我们还年轻，有的是时间和精力。四年后，我们在市中心贷款买了一套100平方米左右的楼房。终于在首府乌鲁木齐市有了一个属于自己的家！

Although my husband had started his own business, I still continued doing my old job and the school distributed one apartment for me in Changji. My family went to live in that apartment every summer and winter vacations after that. The apartment is still there now. After my husband's eldest brother-in-law retired, his family moved to Changji from Qinghe county of Altay, and they lived in the house for four years. In the past, when my husband came to Xinjiang and sought refuge with his relatives, it was this brother-in-law helped him a lot and then he could get the offer from Xinjiang University. Otherwise, our story would not happen, so my husband felt grateful to the brother-in-law all the time, he treated him like his parents.

At that time, my husband put all our money into the stock market and almost lost all our money. He did not know how to operate but just took chance. At last, we only had tens of thousands of RMB left, I asked him to put all the money into his business. The last two years in Geology Team, we rent an apartment near South Railway Station in Urumqi where had convenient transportation. We started a business to make stamps with another fellow folk from Sichuan. In order to make more money, we went to Shanghai to learn how to make stamps on computer instead of making by hand, which would save time and effort. We had to send our son to live with my elder brother during that time.

We rented the cheapest apartment in Shanghai. We went to learnt different skills to save time. I learnt computer operation, and my husband learnt how to fix the machine to make stamps. We used one week and mastered what we need. We only had tens of thousands of RMB left, and no friends and relatives could lend money to us. We bought a stamp machine and a computer desk in Shanghai. This trip to Shanghai made us as poor as Job. But we had confidence, because we were young, we had time and energy. After four years, we paid the down payment and bought a house about 100 square meters in downtown Urumqi. Finally, we had our own home in Urumqi.

* 姐妹情谊

Sister Friendship

上大学时，我与一个同学相处得如姐妹一样。她大学毕业后，在乌鲁木齐市附近的 104 团中学工作。她得知我的情况后，告诉我，抓紧时间调出来，两地分居不好，隐患很多，外面诱惑也多。我那时没有危机感，还觉得过得很舒适，家里有人帮忙做饭，上班也轻松。地质队的水质好，是天山雪水经过

乌鲁木齐市 104 团中学大门（2018）
The Gate of the Middle School of 104 Regiment in Urumqi（2018）

坎儿井引到队里来的，生喝都很甜。蔬菜水果多且新鲜，价格也便宜。后来，她要从 104 团中学调到二十三中，需要我到 104 团中学把她换出来。因为 104 团中学不放她走，必须找个替代老师，所以就找到我。这不是一举两得的事嘛，何乐而不为。

在地质队工作十年之后，我终于从那个几乎与世隔绝的地方调到了大城市附近的兵团。我当时调动很顺利，还以为自己很幸运。后来才知道调进兵团容易，调出去难。我是有经验的骨干教师，学校才同意大学同学调走。

两个月后，大学同学正式调到二十三中。我们还可以见面，凡是市里组织地理教研活动，尤其是每三年一次的继续教育，我们基本上可以碰到。两年后，我也从 104 团中学调到了离家很近的十中，多亏了朋友的善举，我铭记在心！

I had a friend when I was in college, we were like sisters. She worked in a middle school of 104 Regiment near Urumqi after she graduated. She advised me to transfer my job when she knew my situation. She said it was not good for a couple to separate long. There were too many attractions in big city and I should stay together with my husband. But I did not think too much about it. I lived a happy life then and someone could help me cook everyday and my job was easy. Our drinking water was snow water from

Karez. It was sweet. Vegetables and fruits were fresh and cheap. Later, she wanted to transfer to No. 23 Middle School in Urumqi, but 104 Regiment did not let her go unless she could find one who could replace her, so she called me. It was a great news for me, so I was glad to accept it.

I worked in the remote Geology Team for ten years, I moved to a place near big city finally. My job transfer was going smoothly, and I thought I was very lucky. Later, I knew it was easy to transfer into the Corps, but it was hard to get out. I was an experienced and skilled teacher, so they agreed my replacement of my classmate.

Two months later, my friend transferred to No. 23 Middle School. We could meet each other in academic meetings every year and the further education every three years. Two years later, I transferred to No. 10 Middle School where was near my home. I still remember and feel grateful for my friend.

*下定决心
Make up My Mind

　　调到十中不久，侄子来我校上初中。儿子从五年级直接升入初中，没有读六年级。儿子跳级后不久，就出现了英语、数学和语文有点跟不上的问题，我只好抽时间给他补课。空闲之余，想到我藏在心里多年的梦想，准备考研究生，万一我在地质队的"白日梦"成真了呢？碰巧那年是第一年放开研究生考试，不需要单位盖章、领导签字，符合条件就可以报名。我就悄悄报了名，心想如果考上了，就向学校摊牌，考不上也没人知道，不丢人，来年再考，直到考上为止！

　　我下定决心，先自费报了节假日的政治和英语考研辅导班。为了不影响工作，有时候要晚上上课。那时候公婆还在我家，说等我参加完研究生考试之后再回老家，我着实感动了好长时间。他们帮我做家务活，我除了按时上下班之外，就一心一意地复习考研。参

乌鲁木齐市第十中学
The No. 10 Middle School in Urumqi

加完全国研究生统一考试后，公婆准备年底回老家四川，公公满头白发，快 73 岁了。

俗话说，73 岁和 84 岁是人生两大坎。公公相信这些，说要回老家待着，以防万一。公婆都是农村人，没什么文化，但都通情达理，很难得。同事们都以为他们是我的父母，我和他们长得也很像。虽然公婆没有给过我结婚礼物，但是断断续续跟我一起生活了 11 年，帮我照顾孩子、操持家务，我打心眼里感激他们！

Not long after I worked in No. 10 Middle School, my nephew came to my school. My son entered my school after he finished Grade Five in primary school because of his excellent academic performance. But soon after that, my son began to unable to keep pace with English, Math and Chinese. I had to take time to help him with his studies. In my leisure time, I thought of my dream for years, going to the graduate study, maybe my daydream in Geology Team could come true. Fortunately, they made it easier that year. We did not need the recommendation of our working place and did not need the signature from our directors, as long as we were qualified, we could apply for it. I applied secretly. If I passed I would tell my school and if I failed no one would know it. And I would apply again till I passed it.

I made up my mind. I enrolled the tutorial classes for Politics and English in holidays. In order to keep my work normal, I had to take the classes at night sometime. My parents-in-law lived with us at that time, they said they would go back to Sichuan after I took the exam. I was touched for a long time after that. They helped me with housework. Besides my daily work, I only worked on preparing the master entrance exam. After the entrance exam, my parents-in-law prepared to go back to Sichuan. My father-in-law was 72 years old with white hair.

It is said 73 and 84 are two dangerous ages for old people. My father-in-law believes this and he wants to go back his home for his last years. My parents-in-law are both farmers, they are low-educated, but they are very nice. My colleagues all thought they are my parents because we look alike. Although my parents-in-law did not give me any gifts when we got married, they lived with us about eleven years. They helped me take care of my son and do the housework. I feel grateful for them all the time.

* 找到前进的方向
Find a Way Forward

考完研究生的心境与 15 年前考完大学的心情略有不同，事同人非了。我家住七楼，是顶楼，没有电梯，每天大包小包爬上爬下，就当锻炼身体了。上班特忙，这届高三毕业班学生不省心，不如上一届高三毕业班的学生，带得很累，没有动力，更谈不上成就感了。或许是因为教学 15 年，出现了职业倦怠感，感觉大城市的孩子不如地质队的孩子好教，报考研究生隐约有逃避工作的私心在其中。

不久，研究生成绩下来了，英语成绩接近录取线，其他科目都超过了录取分数线，尤其是专业课考得很不错，教学这十几年没有白辛苦，总分也超过录取分数线很多。我报考的是在职研究生，学校有优惠政策，英语成绩录取线可以适当放宽，我就幸运地被录取了。

新疆大学的校园景观（2017）
The Campus Landscape in Xinjiang University（2017）

就在我考上研究生之后，公婆就回四川过年了。我带高三的地理课，寒假需要补课，就没有与他们一起回去。老公开着越野车，送他们回了四川，儿子也跟着回去了，我的内心充满了期待，庆幸自己终于找到了前进的方向。

　　My feeling after the master exam was different from that after the college entrance exam 15 years ago. It was still an exam, but I experienced and grew during the years. My home was on the seventh floor which was the top of the building. There was no elevator in the building. I need climb the stairs every day. I considered it as an exercise. I was very busy that year, I taught Grade Three in high school. The students of this year were hard to teach than the previous class. It made me tired without achievement. It might because I had taught 15 years at school, I felt tired of my career, and also felt students in big city were harder to manage than those in Geology Team. It was also my selfish motives to leave my job.

　　Before long, the exam scores were announced. My English score was close to the admission line. All other scores were much higher than they asked. My more than ten-year teaching helped me a lot. I kept a high level on my academic knowledge. My total score was much higher than what they asked. What I enrolled was the program in the university had a preferential policy. English score can be broadened for who had jobs. I was lucky to be admitted.

After I passed the exam, my parents -in -law went back to Sichuan. I taught Geography for Grade Three in high school, and we had classes in winter vacation, so I could not go back to Sichuan with them. My husband drove them back to Sichuan with my son. I felt lucky to find the right way for my future.

第 3 章　一切皆有可能

Chapter 3　Anything Is Possible

阻碍你的不是你自己不能，而是你认为自己不能。

It's not who you are that holds you back, and it's that you think you're not.

*直面人生
Forced to Face Life

　　我调到 104 团中学之后，公婆与我居住在一起，学校就分给我一个有套间的砖房。房子在学校校园里，很安全。儿子在我们学校对面的小学上学，有公婆照顾。有时，我晚上去老公那儿住，早上再坐公交车去学校上班。早上出门天还没亮，晚上回去天已经快黑了。我每次坐车要两个多小时，中间还要转一次车，很辛苦，但心里很高兴，一家人总算可以天天见面

乌鲁木齐市 104 团中学原教师宿舍（2018）
The Former Teachers' Dormitory of the Middle School of 104
Regiment in Urumqi（2018）

乌鲁木齐市 104 团中学实验楼 (2018)
The Labortory Building of the
Middle School of 104 Regiment
in Urumqi（2018）

了，这就是所谓的且苦且快乐吧！

一年后，我在市里按揭买房，找到离家最近的十中代课，公婆和孩子搬到了新房，儿子转学到新家附近的小学。那时我也不知道哪来的精力，有时一天上午在 104 团中学上课，下午又到十中上课，下班回到家里，嘴巴都僵硬了，一句话都不想说。可是我没有怨言，一心只想着一家人能够团聚。104 团中学领导知道这事后，不同意让我调走。

我想办法找了一个代课老师，才正式调到十中。虽然不是最理想的学校，但是我可以照顾到家和孩子，这就足够了，我也算是个贤妻良母吧！所谓的风雨之后见彩虹，日子是愈过愈好。

After I transferred to the middle school of 104 Regiment, my parents-in-law lived with me. The school distributed me a brick house. The house was in the school, so it was safe. The primary school my son went was across the road from us and my parents-in-law took care of him every day. Sometimes, I went to live with my husband at night and took bus to school next morning. It was dark when I went out in the morning and it was dark when I came back home. It took me more than two hours to take buses and I need change the bus once. It was hard but happy. At least I could stay together with my husband every day.

One year later, I paid the down payment for a new house and I began to teach in No. 10 Middle School which was close to my home. My parents-in-law and my son moved into the new house and my son went to a new primary school. I did not know why I was full of energy at the time. I had classes the whole morning in middle school of 104 Regiment and had classes the whole after-noon at No. 10 Middle School. When I got back home after work, my mouth was stiff, and I could hardly talk. But I did not complain at all. I only wanted my family to get together. After the leaders in middle school of 104 Regiment knew it, they did not al-low me to transfer to another school.

I tried hard and found a substitute teacher, and I became a full-time teacher of No. 10 Middle School after half a year. Al-though it was not my ideal school, it gave me more time to take care of my family. That was enough for me. I deserved the name of good wife. Our life would be better and better.

* 孩子的转变
The Change of Children

　　在十中工作的第二年，父母回了河南老家，和弟弟一起生活。兵团上学的侄子没有人照管，哥嫂工作都忙，就托付给我。侄子成绩不好，学习需要辅导。有哥哥做伴，儿子就想跳级，与哥哥一起读初中一年级。学校已有先例，不少老师的孩子都跳级了，不上六年级，直接升入初中。但需要参加插班考试。虽然儿子考得比侄子好，但作为跳级的条件又差一点。我

乌鲁木齐市第十中学的教学楼
The Teaching Building of No. 10 Middle School in Urumqi

经过深思熟虑后，最终妥协了。虽然存在拔苗助长，影响了孩子的成长，却实现了我的研究生之梦，意想不到的结果！

乌鲁木齐市第十中学运动会（2018）
The Sports Meeting of No. 10
Middle School in Urumqi（2018）

初一第一学期，两个孩子不在同一个班，侄子分到了平行班，儿子分到了英语特色班。不久，初一年级平行班重新组织插班考试，侄子复习功课很努力，分到了平行班中的好班。可是，侄子从小没有养成好的学习习惯，比较调皮。学校课间，有时会被罚站在讲台上。我有时从教室后窗户悄悄观察他的听课情况，时常督促他。一年过去了，侄子总算有些进步了，而儿子的学习成绩却一般。在家里，两个孩子混熟了，他们互相做伴，我也省心一点。儿子上初二时，我考上了新疆大学的在职研究生，与学校签了三年脱产学习的进修合同。

公婆已经回老家，我要负责两个孩子的学习和后勤工作。我终于可以回母校上研究生了。意外的是，我离开学校第一年，侄子学习退步，而儿子的成绩突飞猛进，两个人的表现形成了鲜明的对比。可见，侄子学习不自觉，靠管教；儿子学习

靠自觉。后来才知道，初中后面两年，在我还没下班回家前，两人一起看电视和玩电脑。估计我还有半小时到家，他们就把冰块放在电脑上降温。他们对我的行动了如指掌，学习要是这么用心就好了。

The second year when I worked in No. 10 Middle School, my parents went back to Henan Province and lived with my younger brother. No one could take care of my nephew. My brother and sister-in-law were busy with their work, so I took the job to take care of their son. My nephew did poor in his academic performance and he needed a tutor. With the company of the cousin, my son wanted to be in the same grade with his cousin to middle school. There was precedent at school. Many teachers′ kids skipped Grade Six if they wanted to. They only needed to take an exam and they could go to middle school directly if they passed the exam. My son did better than his cousin in academic performance, but he was not good enough to skip a grade. I turned it over in my mind and I gave up. I agreed him to skip a grade. Maybe it was not good for my son, but it made my dream of being a graduate student come true.

The first semester in middle school, they were not in the same class. My nephew was in a normal class, and my son was in an

English specialty class. Not long, normal classes began an exam to divide classes again. My nephew studied very hard, so he was divided into a better class. But he did not develop a good studying habit and was naughty. He was punished to stand on the platform in the classroom sometimes. I would observe him in the class through the back window and always urged him to study. One year passed, my nephew got some improvement, but my son's performance was only at average level. They accompanied each other at home, so I had more time for myself. When my son was in Junior Two, I became an on-the-job graduate student in Xinjiang University, and I signed a three-year full time study contract with my school.

My parents-in-law had gone to their home, I need take care of the study and life of two boys and finally I could go for my master's study. In my first master year, my son made unexpectedly great improvement in his study, but my nephew could even worse. I found out my son could study conscientiously but my nephew could not. I knew what they did years later that they watched TV and played computer together before I got home. They put ice on computer to cool it down half an hour before I got home every time. They knew my routine very well, I wondered why they did not use their motives in study.

* 心理作用
The Psychological Effect

没想到我的报考志愿没有实现，所报考专业的导师录取人数已满。我报考研究生时，填了可以调剂，所以调剂到另一个女导师名下，但只要能上母校相关专业的研究生，我就很知足了，没有太高的要求。我的研究生导师是一名心理学博士，在外有公职，兼职带新疆大学的研究生。我们调剂的专业是生态学，和生物学相关。我上高中时就比较喜欢生物课，尤其是植物的种类和个体变异这方面的内容，况且我们教育工作者应该学习的职业基础课——教育心理学也是心理学的分支之一，还可以向导师多学些心理学方面的知识，为将来的工作、学习和生活储备知识。

上研一时，每周都有导师的心理学课。导师为我们精心设计教学内容，每次上完导师的课都有很大的收获。那时我的儿子正处在叛逆期，我们经常争吵，偶尔还会有点肢体碰撞。导师知道后，建议我买本《发展心理学》看看，对我会有所帮助。我买了这本书后，边看边实践，一学期快结束时，我和儿子的关系已经缓解了，体现了心理学的作用，同时也要感谢导师的指导。

那时，我对"心理作用"这个心理学词语的学习记忆深刻。比如你买了一件衣服，你自己觉得很好看，但是你的朋友认为不好看，说出了这件衣服的种种缺点，你听了以后，心里就觉得这件衣服确实不好看，这就是心理作用。还记起高考时，我偶感咽喉不舒

新疆大学研究生院
The Graduate School of Xinjiang University

服，母亲就给我买了一瓶黄桃罐头，我吃完以后感觉有所好转，坚持到高考结束。我现在还保留着这个习惯，嗓子感觉不舒服或是有点上火，就立刻买一瓶黄桃罐头，吃完就会感觉好很多，不知道这是否也是心理作用。

如今，有这样一种说法，说穷人买车，富人"买命"；没钱的"抢钱"，有钱的"抢命"。据说有富豪前往乌克兰进行胚胎干细胞抗衰老治疗，这种治疗针一针很贵，富豪们觉得治疗完第二天他们"手脚热乎，甚至视力都好了"，这就是典型的"心理作用"，这种心理暗示带来的作用是不可估量的，尤其是

在防病和治病方面。

I did not expect the major I chose did not accept me because they had enrolled enough students. I circled "Major Adjustable" when I applied, so I became a graduate student of a female professor. She was a doctor in psychology. She worked in the government and was teaching part time at the university. As long as I still could be a graduate student in the university where I got my bachelor's degree, I could accept it happily. My new major was Ecology, and it had some relations with Biology. I liked to take Biology classes in high school, especially the knowledge about species and individual variation of plants. And Educational Psychology, the basic occupational course for all teaching staff, is a part of Psychology. I could learn a lot from my professor which would be a big help for my career.

We had Psychology class every week in the first year. My professor carefully planned every class, we gained greatly. My son was in his rebellious stage then. We always had quarrels and sometimes knocked against each other. My professor suggested me to read Developmental Psychology when she knew it. I bought this book, read it and practiced, till the end of the semester, the relations between my son and I got much better. It was the effect of the psychology, and also I was grateful for my professor's help.

I had a deep memory of the psychological term Psychology Effect. For example, you buy a beautiful coat and you like it very much. But your friend says it is not beautiful and tells you why it is not good. Then you will feel the coat is not good at all. It is Psychology Effect. I got a sore throat when I was taking the College Entrance Exam, so my mother bought me a can of peach. I felt better after I ate it. I keep the habit of eating a can of peach every time when my throat does not well and then I will feel better. I do not know if it is Psychology Effect.

There is news spread these days. It is said that the poor buy the car and the rich buy the life. The poor rob the money, the rich rob the life. It was said that there were billionaires went to Ukraine and received embryonic cell anti-aging treatment. The shot is very expensive. The billionaires felt their hands and feet were warmer, even their sight got better the second day after their treatment. This is the typical Psychology Effect which has enormous effect on treating and preventing diseases.

* 行为归因

Attribution of Behavior

　　研究生导师虽然很忙，但仍认真备课，每堂课都讲得很精彩。尤为可贵的是每次课后，她都留下自学小话题，所涉及的范围较广，如普通心理学、社会心理学等，让我们回家收集资料，确定自己的主题。下次上课时，大家轮流发言，各抒己见，课堂气氛很热烈，效果很好。我在中学给学生上课时，有时也会借鉴导师的教学方法，因材施教，学以致用。这是最好的理论联系实践的做法，上午当学生，下午当老师，这种身份的快速转变，只有身临其境的人才可以体会到其中的乐趣！

　　我印象较深的是一次开放性课题"行为归因"的讨论，我的发言导师比较认可。我是以那些土生土长的四川人作为研究对象，观察到一些四川人与人交往时，不看着别人的眼睛说话，总是往眼下看。我查阅了一些资料，发现这些行为可能与他们小时候的成长环境有关。比如从小在背篓里长大后养成的习惯就是这样的。

　　行为归因是指人们对自己或他人的社会行为进行分析，并指出其性质或推论其原因的过程。都说眼睛是心灵的窗户，与人交往时适时观察对方的眼睛，可以感觉到对方的诚意。说话时眼睛老是回避对方的眼睛，如前面讲到的现象，容易让人产生误解，以至于影响人际交往的效果。归因理论可以用来理解这些与环境相伴随的行为，同时指导人们在日常生活中预测和控制环境，找出行为的原因，从而有效地解决问题。

My professor had her career in the government, but she still spent her time preparing the classes, and every of her class was brilliant. What was more valuable for us was, every time after her class, she gave a small topic, which was in wide range, for example, General Psychology, Social Psychology and so on, let us collect data and identify the focus. We spoke in turn and expressed our own view in next class. It had very good effect. When I taught my students in middle school, I drew on the experience of my professor. It was the best way to link theory with practice of being a student in the morning and being a teacher in the afternoon. The speedy transfer of the identity brought me great pleasure!

The discussion of one open subject about Attribution of Behavior impressed me deeply, my professor accepted my opinion. My objects of study were some people from Sichuan. I found when some of them communicated with each other, they did not look at each other's eyes directly, and they always looked down. I looked up some information, and found that these behaviors might

be related to their growth enviranment since they were little,such as the habits they developed when they grew up in the pack basket.

Attribution of Behavior is the process by which individuals analyze the social behaviors of himself and other people and point out its nature or deduce its cause. It is said eye is the window of one's heart. You can feel his sincerity when he looks into your eyes in the communication. If you always avoid the eye contact in the communication, like what we have mentioned before, it is easy to let people misunderstand and then it would have side effect in your communication. Attribution of Behavior helps you understand the behavior in the different environment and guides you to predict and control the environment and finds the cause to solve the problem.

* 环境心理学
The Environmental Psychology

　　读研究生期间，导师给我们讲授心理学方面的知识，专业课老师给我们讲授生态学方面的内容。对于我来说，专业课是我所熟悉的学科，心理学课程是新的领域。我一方面学习各种心理学的理论知识，另一方面现学现用。市教育局通知所有初三年级都增加地理课，参加中考，并占一定比例的分数。为此，学校让我临时代课一学期。往年初三是没有地理课的，一时学校地理老师不够用，我理应去救急。初三有 10 个班，每个班隔周上一节课，我一周上五节课，把心理学理论知识贯穿于教学中，理论联系实际，收效不错，90%以上的学生都通过了考试，我的教学方式得到了学校领导和老师的认可。

　　导师上课时曾经说过，心理学和我们所学的专业课是有交叉领域的。我通过教学设计活动，并查阅了一些资料，发现有环境心理学之说。虽然有关环境的研究很早就引起了人们的重视，但环境心理学作为一门学科还是 20 世纪 60 年代以后的事情。那时大学课程里还没有这门课，很多人包括一些专业课老师还不了解这个研究领域。70 年代以后，针对环境问题的心理学研究大量出现，同时相关学术杂志、组织和人员也陆续发展

新疆大学的校景 （2018）
The School Scenery of Xinjiang University （2018）

起来，环境心理学研究取得了一些成绩。80 年代和 90 年代，环境心理学已经取得了巨大进步，总体上关于环境问题的心理学研究仍然滞后。

在导师的倡议下，我们积极配合，做了很多工作，写了不少有关环境心理学方面的研究文章，为心理学解决环境问题的研究出了一份力。开展环境心理学研究的现实意义十分明显，社会的需要正是它近年来蓬勃发展的主要动力。

当今环境心理学研究迫切需要贯彻人和自然是和谐统一体的理论思维与价值取向。环境心理学家正在研究可以改变破坏环境行为的方法，到目前为止，只靠教育意义不大，还需要充分挖掘心理学在环境问题的分析与解决上的潜在作用，从环境、经济和社会意义上提高心理学对可持续发展的贡献。

During my master study, my professor taught us Psychological knowledge, professors of professional courses taught us Ecological knowledge. Professional courses were my familiar subject and Psychological courses were a frontier to me. I learned Psychological theories. At the same time, I found chances to practice what I had learned. The Municipal Education Bureau informed all students in Grade Three in junior high schools to take Geography class which took a certain part of scores in senior high school entrance exam. My school asked me to teach the Geography class. Grade Three in previous years did not have Geography class, so there were not enough teachers to teach this course and I should help our school when met the urgent need. There were ten classes in Grade Three, every class had one class every two weeks, so I had five classes each week. I ran Psychological knowledge through my teaching, linked theory with practice. It got a good result. 90% of my students passed the exam and my teaching methods were approved by all leaders and teachers.

My professor once said in the class, there was cross domain between our major and Psychology. I found Environmental Psychology through designing teaching activity and looking up some data. The studies about environment had been taken seriously long time ago, but it was after 1960s since Environmental Psychology became an individual subject. There was no course about this at that time in the university, even a lot of professors did not know much about this subject. In 1970s, a great amount of studies in En-

第３章　一切皆有可能　Chapter 3　Anything Is Possible

vironmental Psychology appeared, and related academic journals, organizations and staff developed at the same time. Environmental Psychology made some progress. In 1980s and 1990s, Environmental Psychology made tremendous progress, but it was still greatly behind other subjects.

Under my professor's initiative, we cooperated actively, and we did a lot work, and wrote many articles about Environmental Psychology and contributed in the study of solving environmental problems. The realistic meaning of developing Environmental Psychology study is significant. The need of the society is the main motive of its booming development.

It is urgent to carry out the theoretical thinking and value orientation of harmonious unity between man and nature in the study of Environmental Psychology nowadays. Environmental Psychologists are studying on how to change the behavior of destroying the environment. It has little significance in relying only on education till now. We need fully develop the potential effect in analyzing and solving environmental problems with Psychology and develop the contribution of Psychology to Sustainable Development from the aspects of environment, economy and social meaning.

*顺势而为

Follow the Situation

　　36 岁时，我考上了新疆大学资源与环境科学学院的研究生，是当时那一届招收的研究生中年龄最大的学生，刷新了历年来的最高纪录，据说之前最大年龄是 33 岁。但是我在新生见面会上并不显老，不做自我介绍，大家还以为我和他们是一样的应届毕业生呢，好好地"虚荣"了一次。我的心态好像又

新疆大学原地理系教学楼一角（2018）
The Corner of the Former Teaching Building in Department of Geography of Xinjiang University（2018）

回到了大学时代。说心里话，不用上班有一种解脱的感觉。工作 15 年，可能是到了职业疲劳期，该充电了，否则会被时代淘汰。

我非常珍惜上天给我的这次难得的学习机会，学习起来比其他研究生都认真。我不放过任何一次参加学习和活动的机会，用"如饥似渴"来形容都不为过。师弟师妹们不理解我，说我有好的工作，生活不是挺好的嘛，为什么还要吃苦。这可能就是代沟吧！他们认为学习是受苦，而我却相反，觉得是一件愉快的事情。学习比上班强多了，不用早上签到，面临经常查岗；备课付出很多心血，学生却不用心听课，经常有一种挫败感。这些他们不理解，将来他们面临的挑战比我们这一代要严峻得多。

新疆大学硕士毕业要求英语成绩至少达到学校规定的六级分数线之上。全国统一研究生英语六级考试都在下午三点以后，正是我打瞌睡的时候，所以考试成绩总是不理想。我参加了三次六级英语考试，一次好过一次。最后一次复习的强度最大，早起背英文单词，下午强化练习，考试时不吃饭，只吃点巧克力，补充能量，因为吃多了，就会打瞌睡，影响考试成绩。功夫不负有心人，最后考试成绩终

新疆大学的校园之路（2018）
The Campus Road of
Xinjiang University（2018）

于达到学校的硬性要求，硕士研究生顺利毕业了。

三年的研究生收获很多，结交了很多现在还联系的师弟师妹。而且还见到很多上大学时教过我的老师们，与他们切磋学术，受益匪浅。我的初衷是学习自然地理学，可以促进教学，还有利于职称评定。快毕业时，我遇见大四时的班主任。他已经是教授，可以带博士研究生了，招收的专业是自然地理学。他得知我的遗憾，就建议我考他的博士研究生，我说试试吧。

没想到，博士入学考试比硕士简单得多，我顺利通过了考试。我估计与学校谈判比较难，但只要能让我读博士，再苛刻的条件我都答应。在签订硕士进修协议之后，我又和十中续签了博士进修协议。除了违约金高些，还被要求每周上八九节高中地理课，相当于满工作量的一半。对我来说，这都不是问题。能够硕博连读，让我有点膨胀。殊不知考进容易毕业难，往后的三年确实使我磨炼了意志，开阔了眼界！

I got the offer from Xinjiang University and became a graduate student of the College of Resource and Environmental Science when I was 36 years old. I was the oldest student of that year. The record age was 33 before me. I did not look old among the new students. Others all thought I was as young as a college student before I introduced myself which gratified my vanity. I was like going back to my college time. I felt myself was free from the work. Fif-

teen-year working time made me tired of the job, so I need leave and recharge for a new stage of the work.

I valued the studying chance very much this time. I worked much harder than all other graduate students. I did not miss any opportunity of studying and activity. I absorbed all the knowledge like a sponge. All other graduate students did not understand me. In their mind, I had a good job and lived a better life than them, why did I choose to come back to study again. Maybe it was the gap between the ages. They thought study was hard, but it was a pleasure for me to have a chance to study again. Studying is much better than working. I did not need to sign in in the morning and did not need to face the leaders´ check from time to time. I spent a lot of time preparing the class but students did not pay any attention to it which made me frustrated. My young classmates did not understand what they would face in the future might be more serious than ours.

A master student must pass CET-6 exam in Xinjiang University. CET-6 exam always held after 3pm which was my sleepy time. Because of this, I took the exam for three times. What made me happy was my grade was better and better each time. Especially the last time, I recited English words in the morning and did exercises in the afternoon. I did not have lunch except some chocolates on the exam day. I knew I would be sleepy if I ate too much. Finally, I met the requirement and graduated successfully.

My three-year graduate study had yielded good results. I made friends with many younger classmates and still in connections now. I also discussed and learned academic knowledge from my college teachers there. The original intention of studying Natural Geography was to help my teaching in middle school and to benefit the professional title appraisal. Right before my graduation, I met my tutor when I was senior in college. He had become a professor then, and he could tutor doctoral students of Natural Geography major. He understood my desire and encouraged me to start my doctoral study. I told him that I would try.

Unexpectedly, doctoral entrance exam was much easier than that of master, and I passed it without doubt. I guessed it was hard to negotiate with the school I worked. But as long as I could start my doctoral study, I could accept all their requirements. Then I signed a further study contract with No. 10 Middle School. Besides a high penalty, I was asked to give eight Geography classes in high school each week, which was the half of a full-time teaching load. There was no problem for me at all as long as I could continue my study. I felt swelling of starting the doctoral study, but I did not expect it was hard to graduate. The following three years strengthened my mind and broadened my views.

* 实现梦想

Fulfill My Dreams

　　人活在世上只有短短的几十年。对于 20 世纪 60 年代末出生的我来说，只有 6 岁以前是无忧无虑的童年，之后的小学、初中、高中和大学前后 15 年都在上学学习。大四的时候，我参加了研究生考试，差几分没有被录取，上研究生成了我的梦想。大学毕业后，我的爱好一直没有变，还是喜欢英语，可以说是百看不厌，每天不看一点英语就好像少了什么东西似的，但是听力和口语较差，可能是训练得太少。

　　第一年工作时，刚出学校，可以教初三英语，顺带教初中地理。因为我所学的专业和地理相关的，涉及职称评定，要求专业对口，后来只能教地理。这一教就是 15 年，只是换了 4 个不同的学校而已。工作 15 年后，我已经 36 岁了。我始终不忘初心，参加了全国研究生统一考试，考入新疆大学资源与环境科学学院。在职进修硕博连读 6 年后，由博士导师及相关专家推荐，有幸进入北京师范大学环境学院博士后流动站，与合作导师共同从事环境科学研究，两年后顺利出站。这样算下来，我这短短的前半生，有一大半时间是在读书、学习及研究中度过。

读书有三层境界。读书的第一层境界：一心读书，只为考试。为了考试而读书，真正的目的不在于读书，而是在于考试的结果，在于考试背后的利益，比如我最初考大学就是为了毕业后离开兵团。读书的第二层境界：行万里路，读万卷书。便是摆脱书本的束缚，在实践中体会书中的情理与意境，比如我的研究生学习及实践。读书的第三层境界：找到自己，读懂人生。在读书的最高境界中，你知道了自己想要什么东西，想成为什么样的人，该做什么事情，并且会努力地去实现。

　　有人说："读书和旅行一样，可以在别人的世界里寻找自己。"在读书中，你可以经历一千种人生，然后在其中发现自己的人生。

　　亚里士多德说："人的最高价值在于觉醒与思考的能力，而不在于生存本身。"

新疆大学图书馆（2018）
The Library of Xinjiang University（2018）

读书的最终目的，便是帮我们获得这种觉醒与能力。让人按照自己的意愿活下去，才是读书最高的价值。

我的这些经历是自己这辈子都始料未及的，可以说是梦想成真，而且远远地超出了我最初的梦想。我以后的生活目标就是逐步进入读书的最高境界，实现读书最高的价值！

有些事情只要你认定能做，就要坚持下去，就一定会达到自己预期的目的，甚至可能会超出预期。不信的话，你可以尝试一下。

Everyone has only several decades in this world. My childhood was joyous and carefree before I was six years old for I was born in the late 1960s. In the following fifteen years, there was only study in my life. I entered the master entrance exam when I was a senior student, but I failed to pass the exam. After I graduated from the college, I still loved English very much. It seemed something was missing if I did not read English each day, but my listening and speaking were still not good for the lack of practice.

The first year I worked, I taught English for Grade Three and Geography for Grade One to Grade Three in middle school. Because my major is related to Geography, and for the sake of professional title appraisal, I had to teach Geography class only. In fifteen years, I changed four schools but always as a Geography teacher. I was already 36 years old when I decided to take the master entrance exam. I entered the College of Resources and Environmental Science of Xinjiang University for my master and doctoral study. Then with the recommendation of my professor and some experts, I went to Post-doctoral Mobile Station of School of Environment of Beijing Normal University and cooperated with my professors to do the study on Environmental Science. I successfully left the Post-doctoral Mobile Station two years later. In the first half of my life, I had spent more than half of time in studying.

There are three states in reading. The first state of reading is reading for tests only. Reading for taking test is for the result of tests and for the benefits of tests other than for reading itself. My purpose of going to college was to leave the small place I grew up. The second state of reading is traveling far and reading more. That is to get rid of the book's bound and experience the book's emotion and artistic conception in practice, such as my graduate study and practice. The third state of reading is finding yourself and understanding your life. In this last state of reading, you will know what you want to have, what you want to be, what you should do and try your best to achieve it.

Someone said, "Reading is like traveling, you can find yourself in other people's world. " You can experience one thousand people's life in reading and then find yours in it.

Aristotle said, "The highest value of human lies in the ability of awakening and thinking, not in the survial itself. "

The ultimate purpose of reading is to help us get the awareness and the power. It is the ultimate value of reading when people can live on his will.

My experiences are unexpected. I can tell my dreams have come true and even surprised me much more compared with my initial dreams. The goal of my life will be entering the highest state of reading and achieve the ultimate value of reading.

Once you decide to do something, you should stick on it, then you must achieve what you expect, maybe you can do better. Please give yourself a chance and have a try.

第 4 章　引导之路

Chapter 4　A Guiding Way

成长并实现自己的梦想是需要勇气的。

It takes courage to grow up and make your dream come true.

*中考生的告白

Examinee's Confession

　　那时，兵团连队的学生如果考不上大学，就基本上在家种地，过着那种"面朝黄土，背朝天"的生活。可想而知，家长的压力有多大，当父母的都不希望自己的孩子过那种生活。我的母亲也一样，虽然我们家已经搬到团部，不住在连队，但是考不上大学一样会去种地。

　　从我家院子门口到我住的小隔间距离比较长，中间隔着棚子和厨房。我一放学，除了吃饭，就是学习。母亲经常在棚子里干活。有同学来找我，她就要先看同学的手上是否拿有书本，如果没有，她就认为是来找我玩的，肯定说

第七师 127 团团部中学（2008）
The Regimental Middle School in the 127 Regiment of the 7th Division（2008）

我不在家。

记得中考前三天，有一位女同学拿着书本敲我家门，母亲自然放她进来了。这位女同学长得很漂亮，但学习成绩比较差。我那时只顾学习，想抓紧时间给她讲题，她拿来的是物理题和数学题，要求我把答案写下来，说想回家再琢磨一下。她问的题目都是我最近才见过的题型，完全不在话下，一会儿我就搞定了。她心满意足地走了。

大哥考上中专学校走后，留下不少学习资料，我全都认真地做了一遍，包括各科老师发的复习资料。我心里很踏实，自信心十足，就等着考试了。第一天考数学时，发现不少题目似曾相识。当时没想那么多，挥笔就做，一气呵成，感觉爽啊！第二天考试，物理题目也出现了这种感觉，好像都见过似的。我回家后仔细一想，突然想起来了，考前那个女同学曾经来问过题的，还要求我把答题过程写下来，她都带走了。

难道中考题目泄露出去了吗？我这方面的思维迟钝，不能确定是否是巧合，就把这件事原原本本地告诉母亲了。母亲一听，第一个反应就是叫我不要乱说，说出去那个女生的一生就毁了。况且，你也没有证据，就当自己模拟考试了一次。我想也是，至少考试时很轻松。

我是班里的学习委员，学习成绩一直名列前茅。听说那个女生考上了团部高中，只是成绩刚好过线，有没有人怀疑她，我就不知道了。我当什么也没发生，我们也没有分在一个高中班，基本上很少见面。后来得知那个女生没有读完高中就嫁人了，估计是漂亮"惹的祸。"

Then, we, who belonged to the company of the Corps, were destined to do farm work at home if we could not go to college. Face to the ground and back to the sky, that would be the life of our whole life. Parents did not want their kids copy their life again and they undertook much pressure, so did my mother. Although my family had moved to the regimental headguarters, we did not live in the company anymore, I still would go back to work in the Corps if I could not go to college.

There was some distance from the gate to my room, a barn and a kitchen were between them. I only had two things to do after school, eating and studying. My mother was always working in the barn. Every time my classmates came to our house, she would check whether they had books in their hands. If they did not take books with them, she would firmly believe they came to play with me, so she would tell them I was not at home.

Three days before the final exam, a girl came with her books, so my mother let her in. She was a beautiful girl, but she did bad in her study. She asked me to write the answers of those Physics and Math questions she took to me and she could think about the answers when she went back home. The questions were all my familiar types and I just wanted to save my time, so I wrote down the answers quickly and she left happily.

After my eldest brother went to the technical secondary school, he left me many learning materials. I reviewed them all including the materials the teachers handed out. I was full of confidence for the exam. It was Math on the first day, and I found many questions familiar. I answered quickly and happily. The second day, I had the same feeling on Physics. There were too many questions I thought I had met before. After the Physics test, I remembered suddenly, the girl came to ask me these questions, and she asked me to write down answers and she took them away.

Were the exam papers leaked? I was slow in thought about this and could not be sure whether it was just a coincidence, so I told it to my mother. My mother stopped me from telling it to other people immediately. She said I did not have the evidence and it would ruin the girl's life. She asked me to consider it as a practice test. I convinced myself and it made me relaxed in the exam.

I was the commissary in charge of studies and always among the best in exams in our class. But later I heard that girl met the requirements of high school in the regimental headquarters. I did not know if anyone ever doubted about the scores. We were not in same class in the high school and I acted like nothing happened between us. I heard she quitted school and got married. Someone said it was because of her pretty face.

*高考志愿
College Application

　　高考完，我感觉发挥得不好，变得乖巧了很多。我从小就是个很听话的孩子，敬畏和崇拜母亲。填报高考志愿都是按照母亲让我学医的要求做的，从重点院校到中专院校，全都填满了，只有重点院校参考志愿里的第二个志愿没有填报医学院，因为没有找到合适的学校，就填了新疆大学。

　　在这之前，我大哥的一个女同学（母亲同事的女儿）曾经考上这所大学，母亲在我耳边念叨了好久，所以就顺手填上了。因为喜欢英语和生物，就填报了外语系和生物系。母亲满意了，我就递交上去了，等待命运的安排。结果我却被新疆大学地

新疆大学原地理系教学楼的门口（2018）
The Doorway of the Former Teaching Building in the
Department of Geography of Xinjiang University（2018）

第 4 章　引导之路　Chapter 4　A Guiding Way

理系录取了。当时只要考上大学，学校都给予适当地奖励，母亲也只好顺其自然。

俗话说得好，有失必有得。高考完以后，我老老实实在家待着。拿到录取通知书，就听母亲说表舅要结婚了，要她去帮忙，刚好我也没什么事情了，就陪母亲去新疆哈密市看望大哥和表舅，顺便帮忙收拾新房。然后直接去乌鲁木齐新疆大学报到，就不回兵团的家了。表舅结完婚之后，我稍微清闲了些。有一天，偶然去了一趟医院。还没到医院，我远远地就闻到了医院福尔马林的味道，胃里就开始翻腾，差一点就要呕吐了，都没有办法走进医院，心里暗自庆幸自己没有学医！

I knew I did not do well in college entrance exam, so I became well-behaved at home. I was an obedient child all the time, I regarded my mother with reverence. I followed my mother´s instruction in medical major to fill the form from key universities to technical secondary schools. I did not choose medical major for the second application in key university. I did not find a right school, so I wrote Xinjiang University.

One of my big brother´s classmates who was also the daughter of my mother´s colleague, studied in Xinjiang University. My mother always talked to me about it, so I wrote it in the application form. I like English and Biology, so I chose the major of English and Biology. My mother was satisfied with my application, and then I submitted the form and waited for the result. Finally, I got an offer from the Department of Geography of Xinjiang University. At that time, as long as we could get an offer from a university, local middle school would give a reward to the student, so my mother did not comment.

It is said one cannot make an omelet without breaking eggs. I stayed at home after the college entrance exam. Till I received the offer from Xinjiang University, my mother said she would go and help on my uncle's wedding. I went with my mother to Hami to visit my eldest brother and uncle there and then I could go to the university directly. After my uncle's wedding, I had a few days free time. One day, I need go to hospital. But before I went into the hospital, I smelled a strong smell of formalin which made me feel sick. I could not go into the hospital that time and I felt lucky that I did not get any offer from medical major.

* 大学生活
College Life

进大学时，我只有 16 岁半。班里一个最小的男生，进校时个子很小，大学毕业时，长到了一米八。毕业那年他是我们的班长，可以说，大学四年我们的身心都在成长。班里还有两个同学，一个男生和一个女生，都比我小两个月。巧合的是，他们俩竟然是同年同月同日生，像是小说里写的一样，可是，他们四年没有发生恋情。这个男生是我大学里的"四人组合"之一，他会下围棋，是我的师傅。遗憾的是，直到毕业我也没有出师。因为我深知自己的目标是考研究生，棋类活动只是我的爱好而已。

大二结束时，我荣获一等奖学金 150 元，给母亲买了一件裘皮大衣，花去 70 元，剩下的就作为生活费了。后来，母亲调到团部罐头厂做销售工作，干得很好，经常去内地出差，推销罐头，原料主要是吐

我的入校照（1985）
My College Photo（1985）

鲁番的葡萄。她出差时，经常给我带些葡萄罐头等。如果去吐鲁番采购葡萄，我就请假跟着去。回来时，顺便带些新鲜葡萄给室友们尝尝，吐鲁番的葡萄真是名不虚传。

我的奖学金证书
My Scholarship Certificate

我在班里年龄比较小，还处于懵懵懂懂状态，答应母亲四年不谈男朋友。大学期间基本上做到了与男同学和平相处，只讲同学情谊，不谈个人感情。大学四年，我的学习成绩总体上属于中偏上水平。本以为靠自己的勤奋努力就可以达到自己的目标，可是事与愿违，大四时参加全国研究生考试，结果差几分没有上线，心里的失落感可想而知。这个心结也就在那个时候深埋在心里。

I was only sixteen years old when I went to the college. The

我读大学时的教学楼（2018）
The Teaching Building in my College years（2018）

youngest boy in our class was the shortest one and he grew to almost 6 feet four years later. He was the monitor of our class in the
fourth year. We grew much both physically and mentally during
those four years. There was a boy and a girl in our class, who were
two months younger than me. How lucky, they were born in the
same day just like what always happened in the novel. But there
was no love story happened between them. The boy was one
member in my Group-of-Four in college. He can play Weiqi, so he
taught me. I did not play it well till I graduated. I knew my goal
was to go to master school, and Weiqi was only a hobby.

I earned 150 RMB scholarships at the end of the second year.

I spent 70 and bought my mother a fur coat, the rest was my daily expenses. Later, my mother became a sales person in a can company, and she did very good in her job. She always went to other provinces to promote their canned fruit which was made of Turpan grapes. She always brought me their canned grapes when she came to see me. Turpan grapes are the best. I would go with her when she went to purchase grapes in Turpan. And I brought grapes back to my roommates.

I was younger than most of my classmates, so I was not as mature as them. I promised not to have boyfriend during my college life. I got along at peace with all male classmates during those four years. We were in good friendship without personal affections. My academic performance was above the average in those four years. I thought I could achieve my goal through my hard work. But it went contrary to my wishes. I took the master entrance exam and I failed with only a few scores less. It made me so upset and it rooted in my heart deeply for a long time.

*向党靠拢

Move toward the Communist Party

　　硕士考试的复试即将开始，我准备得很充分，带着考试用具提前来到考场。突然听到有人问，是董老师吗？一抬头，看见是我在地质队曾经教过的一个女学生，她的名字我还记得，因为那时她表现比较突出，如今都长成大姑娘了，但还是中学时的模样，没有多大变化。我们简单地聊了几句。复试完，我们都被录取了，分在不同的导师名下。

　　英语课和政治课是公共课，我们所有研究生都在一起上课，会经常见面。我们有时还坐在一起聊聊当年的学生和老师，他们的去向和情况，她知道的还不少。她是我们这一届研究生的支部书记，时间长了，她就动员我入党。我的两个哥哥都是党员，我也要要求进步，不能落后，就积极写入党申请书。

　　我们曾是师生关系，但是现在转变成了同学关系。一视同仁，我与其他入党积极分子一样，首先需要经常写思想汇报，定期汇报自己的学习情况和思想动态，然后交给她。她成了我的入党介绍人之一。

　　然后就是定期上党课。每次上完党课，都要回去写心得体会，下次课前交上去，然后继续写心得体会，直到考完试为止。入党积极分子培训考试是闭卷考试，而且很严格。我下了很大的功夫，考试成绩不错。同学们都知道我的年龄，确实给大家做了榜样。

毕业之际，我光荣地加入了中国共产党，成为了一名预备党员，一年后转正。入党宣誓的情景历历在目，是我一生中最难忘的一幕。有人说入党是为了当官，否则没有什么用。而我却不赞同，每个人的信仰不同，"三观"不同，所以有"物以类聚，人以群分"之说。走自己的路，让别人说去吧！

The second turn of master entrance exams was coming soon. I made full preparation for it and arrived at the examination room early. Suddenly someone called me, "Are you Teacher Dong?" I looked up and saw a girl whom I taught when I worked in the school of Geology Team. I still remembered her name. She was an outstanding student then. She grew up a lot, but she still had a young face like when she was in middle school. We chatted a little bit. After the exams, we both got the offer but under different professors.

English and Politics were public courses, so all graduate students took these two classes together and we always met each other. We sometimes talked about teachers and students in the previous school and she knew much about their information. She was the Party secretary for masters enrolled that year. She encouraged me to join Communist Party as we got along with each other more. Both my brothers were members of Communist Party. I thought I could not fall behind so I wrote the application letter of joining the Communist Party.

I was her teacher at first, but then she became my classmate. She treated me the same as other activists. We need write on our study and thought report regularly, then handed to her. She became one of my sponsors when I applied for Party membership.

We had regular party classes. We need write about what we had learnt and understood after each class and handed it in next class till the semester ended. We had a strict exam for the party member training class. I studied very hard and finally I got a good score on it. My classmates all knew I was much older than them, and I made a good example for them.

I became a probationary Party member right before I graduated, and I became a Party member one year later. It was the most unforgettable scene in my life when I took the oath and became a member of Communist Party. Someone said it was useless to be a Party member if you do not want to make achievements in government. I do not agree with it. Everyone has his own belief and faith that others do not understand. Follow your own course, and let people talk.

*博士经历

Experience of the Doctoral Study

　　在与学校签订硕博连读的协议后，我心里有点没底气。因为博士导师是自己的大学班主任，心里稍微安定了些。一方面我的教学工作不能耽误，每周要上九节高中地理课。另一方面，儿子的高中学习也不能松懈。我早早地做好了博士学习的计划，任何与读博相关的事情都尽量往前赶。

　　读博第一年，在完成专业基础课和公共课学习的基础上，我参阅大量的文献资料，准备发表论文的初稿，并琢磨开题报告的选题。选题的确定反复与导师商量，几个提议和方案导师都不太满意，觉得不够前沿。在一个师弟的建议下，最后，我确定做大气模式和水文模型的耦合研究。这在当时可是热点问题。

　　读博第二年，学校要求选修一门二外。我选了日语，一学期后通过了考

新疆大学的校门（2018）
The Gate of Xinjinag University（2018）

试。按照要求完成了开题报告，接着，在中文核心期刊上发表了两篇论文，只剩下毕业论文。

首先，学习水文模型 SWAT。我的一个师弟是一个博士研究生，他以前做过这个水文模型，开题报告的主题就是这个师弟给的建议。我跟着师弟学了一个星期，从安装到运行，整个流程都认真地学习和操作。这个模型需要进一步研发，比较有发展前景，也是我比较喜欢做的模型。后来，博士导师推荐我进博士后流动站继续深入地研究它。

第二步，学习大气模式。我每天除了上课，剩下的时间几乎都是去气象局学习区域气候模式 RegCM3。因为历年的气象数据占有的空间较大，所以要求电脑的配置较高才可以运行。老公很支持我，在电脑城的朋友处租了一台硬盘 500G 的台式电脑，用来运行大气模型。气象局的一位女研究员是这个气候模型的专家，做了很多年研究。我跟着学习，避免了走弯路，

新疆大学的逸夫楼（2010）
The Yifu Building of
Xinjiang University（2010）

很快就掌握了要领。我心里一直感激这位研究员的帮助。在读博的路上，虽然遇到了一些困难，但总是有贵人相助，逢难化易。

那时我的干劲不知道怎么那么大，为了安装模型，我可以整晚不睡觉，模型的运行需要时间，要及时输入相应的数据，还要输出对应的结果。如果出现问题，就需要调整参

数，再重新运行，反复试验，直到达到预期的效果。那段时间，我经常拎着手提电脑，往返于家和气象局之间，有时回来晚了，来不及做饭，就叫儿子到外面的餐馆吃。

新疆大学校园（2017）
The Campus of
Xinjiang University (2017)

记得有一天，我在家写论文，一时忘了锅里煮着白水蛋，直到听到锅里有叮咚的声音，才反应过来，赶紧冲向厨房，看见锅里的鸡蛋正在"跳舞"，鸡蛋外皮已经发黄了，但还可以吃。上高中的儿子放学回来看到鸡蛋皮是黄的，很奇怪。我说了原因，他让我以后做饭时不要写论文，否则很危险。我也是这样认为的，要么专心写论文，要么专心做饭。从此以后，再没有发生类似的事情。

读博第三年，儿子考上了大连大学。他上学走后，我更是加班加点地写毕业论文，投稿在中文核心期刊的第三篇论文也顺利发表了。这一年在忙忙碌碌中度过，有苦也有乐。最大的成功就是博士答辩顺利通过，师生狂欢到半夜，还给母亲打电话，激动得声音都有点颤抖了，告诉她我博士毕业了。

I signed the contract of my master and doctor study with my previous school, but I did not have the confidence. My doctoral professor was the professor taught me when I was in college which made me feel better. I had nine classes to teach in the previous middle school each week. And I also need make much effort on my son´s high school study. I made a detailed plan for my doctoral study and I tried to finish everything in advance.

In the first year of my doctoral study, besides finishing the academic and public courses, I made much effort on literature review for the first draft of my paper and thinking of the topics of the paper. I discussed several times with my professor about my paper topic, but he was not satisfied with all of them because he thought my topics were not innovative enough. Under the suggestion of one younger schoolmate, I finally decided to do the paper on the coupling of atmospheric model and hydrological model which was a hot topic at that time.

In the second year, we were required to choose one foreign language besides English to learn. I chose Japanese and passed the exam at the end of the semester. I also passed the paper proposal on time and had two publications on the key academic journals. The only thing left was my thesis.

First of all, I need learn the Hydrological Model SWAT. One of my younger schoolmates was a doctoral student. He once made the hydrological model and it was him who suggested me to do it. I learned one week on installing and operating from him. I studied and operated the whole process carefully. The models need further research and development. It had great developing prospect and it was the model I liked. Later, my professor recommended me to study and do further research on it in the Post-doctoral Mobile Station.

Second, learn atmospheric model. I spent all my rest time learning Regional Climate Model RegCM3 in Meteorological Bureau after school every day. Because the meteorological data took much space, it required a high configuration of computer. My husband supported me and rent a computer with 500G space from his friend for me to run the atmospheric model. A female researcher from the Meteorological Bureau was an expert on this model and she studied it for many years. I began to learn from her and I mastered the essentials quickly. I felt grateful for her help all the time. I met some difficulties in my doctoral study, but there were always people helped me out.

I did not understand why I was so energetic all the time then. I could stay up the whole night for installing the model. Model operation need time, related data should be input in time and corresponding result should be output. If there was anything wrong, parameters should be adjusted, operation should be done again, tests should be done ever and ever again to get the expected result. I held the laptop and went and came between home and Meteorological Bureau nearly every day. I had to go out and eat with my son if I came home too late to cook sometimes.

One day, I was working on my thesis and forgot there were eggs boiled in the pot. Suddenly I heard some cracking noise. I rushed to the kitchen, and I saw eggs dancing in the pot and shells turned brown. I tasted one and it was still ok to eat. My son felt curious about the brown egg shell. I told him what I had done. He asked me to not work on the thesis when I cooked. I thought so and I did not do it again.

The third year, my son got the offer from Dalian University. I spent more time on my thesis after he went to college. And the third paper was published on a key academic journal. It was a busy year for me with happiness and sadness. The happiest thing was I passed the oral defense of my graduation thesis. All of us got wild in the party. I called my mother and told her I became Dr. Dong with my shaky voice.

* 催化剂

Activator

在我读博二的时候，工作的单位换了校长。新校长是我的校友，数学系毕业的，比我低两届。她很好强，说如果当时她是校长，绝对不会同意我去读博士的，一个中学是留不住博士的。幸亏当时她还没有调来，这就是天意。博士毕业后我回到单位全职上课，同事们不理解我，我不在乎，因为我心里有期待，这是个秘密。

回到单位工作的第一个学期，我全身心地投入到地理教学中，经常加课，自习课几乎都被我占用了。上了一学期的课，感觉像上了一年的课似的。工作量都是我自己加上去的。学校领导给我申请了一个高级职称的额外指标。博士学历直接晋升高级职称符合国家政策。但这在我所在的中学是一个先例，必须完成所有评审程序，参加计算机培

乌鲁木齐市第十中学的大门（2018）
The Gate of No. 10 Middle School in Urumqi（2018）

家里外面阳台上的鲜花（2018）
Flowers on the Balcony
outside of the House（2018）

训、考核及发表论文的答辩。我认真对待，因为这个机会来之不易，有多少老师羡慕不已。冰心说："成功的花，人们只惊羡她现时的明艳，然而当初她的芽儿，渗透了奋斗的泪泉，洒遍了牺牲的血雨。"这是我的心声，没有人能够体会。

我博士毕业的时候，博士导师已经帮我联系了北京师范大学环境学院的博士后流动站，建议我进站继续研究我喜欢的水文模型SWAT。那年我43岁，我在网上查了一下，了解到北京师范大学环境学院流动站的招生，要求年龄原则上不超过40岁，我有些纠结。博士导师鼓励和支持我，他很自信，说肯定会有支援边疆建设的指标，我决定尝试一下。

单位肯定不会再与我签订任何协议了，校长极力劝我留下来，协助她管理学校，但这些都不是我想要的。与我共事的一个物理老师，比我大两三岁，她说45岁是女人青春的尾巴，你一定要抓住，否则后悔一辈子。这无疑是给我打了一针催化剂。是啊，人一生只有一个45岁，我要抓住青春的尾巴再折腾一次，不要做让自己后悔的事。现在看来，是正确的时间做出了正确的选择。

In the second year of my doctoral study, my working school had a new president, who was my schoolmate in Xinjiang University. She was from Math Department and two levels below me. She was a strong-willed woman. She said she would not allow me to go on the doctoral study if she was there then, because no doctor would like to stay and teach in a middle school. I felt I was so lucky she was not the president then. After I got my doctor's degree, I still went back to the previous school. My colleagues did not understand me. I did not care. I had an expectation in my heart, and that was my secret.

The first semester I went back to work, I devoted myself to the Geography class teaching. I always gave extra classes, even the self-study class was taken over by me. One semester's teaching made me tired like I taught the whole year. It was me who put so much extra load on myself. My school applied an extra senior professional title for me, because the doctor degree could apply the senior title directly according to the policy. I was the first people who had doctor degree in middle school. I must finish all judging process, take computer training and test, and pass the paper defense. It was an opportunity hard to win. Many teachers admired me, and I was proud of myself. Bingxin said, "People only admire the blooming flower's beauty. No one cares how much effort it makes and how much tears it sheds into the earth when it was a sprout. " People only admired me, but no one knew how much hard work I had done.

When I got graduated, my professor had recommended me to continue my study on Hydrological Model SWAT in the Post-doctoral Mobile Station of School of Environment of Beijing Normal University. I was 43 years old that year. I searched on the website of the Post-doctoral Mobile Station. In principle, they only enrolled people who were under 40 years old. I was struggled about it and my professor encouraged me. He was confident about they must have the quota for supporting frontier construction. I decided to make a try.

My school refused to sign any contract with me, the president persuaded me to stay and help her to take charge of the school. But this was not what I wanted. One teacher, who taught Physics, was two or three years older than me. She said 45 was the end of a woman's best time, you must grab it otherwise you would regret in the rest of your life. What she said was an activator to me. How many 45 years could I have. I must grab the tail of the best age and do not let myself regret. It now seems I made the correct choice at a correct time.

*不懈努力
Unremitting Efforts

　　我如愿以偿地来到北京师范大学环境学院，找到我的合作导师，与他商量进站事宜。按照北京师范大学博士后流动站的进站要求，至少需要两位相关专业教授的推荐信才能进站。除了博士导师，还有一位资源与环境科学学院的教授为我写了推荐信。很快收到了中国博士后网站提示预约的短信，我就去北京办理相关进站手续。我很佩服博士导师的判断力，立刻就把好消息告诉了他。他很高兴，希望我努力配合合作导师做项目，完成自己的愿望，不留遗憾。人这一生能有一个懂自己的恩师实属不易，前世修来的福！

　　我进北京师范大学环境学院博士后流动站后不久，合作导师申请到一个973项目，成为青年科学家。他的硕士生都要发表一篇影响因子2.0以上的外文期刊才能毕业，何况我一个博士后。合作导师找了两个博士帮助我，他们的专长与我的研究领域相关，我的信心大增，继续琢磨用于环境科学研究的水文模型SWAT。

　　按照北京师范大学博士后流动站的出站要求，我计划两年出站，要在正式刊物上发表学术论文两篇，还要发表一篇影响

第4章　引导之路　Chapter 4　A Guiding Way

北京师范大学环境学院门口（2012）
The Gate of Environmental Department
of Beijing Normal University（2012）

因子 2.0 以上的外文期刊。我要发表在中文期刊的文章已经准备好，投稿、接收和发表都没有问题。关键是 SCI 的写作，影响因子 2.0 以上对于我来说要求有些高了。初期的写作总是达不到合作导师的要求，几次想打退堂鼓，都被老公说服了。

我在北京师范大学住了一段时间，上网查阅了相关的英文期刊，学习作者的写作技巧。有一次我向帮我调到 104 团中学的那个大学同学求救，因为她的语文水平比较高，想让她帮我看看中文，然后再翻译成英文。告诉她因为写不出符合合作导师要求的论文前言，都想跳楼了。她却说，她不懂我的专业，不可能帮我看中文。让我记住，在跳楼之前，先要长出翅膀。我彻底觉醒了，只有自己靠得住！

从此以后，我加倍努力，头发掉得很厉害。一年后，在所有人尤其是合作导师和他推荐的两个博士的帮助下，当然还有老公的鼎力支持，才有了 SCI 文章的雏形。半年后，我的 SCI 论文正式发表，同时还完成了出站报告。两年后，我顺利出站。合作导师想挽留我，说我写作 SCI 已经有经验，让延期一年再出站。我没有同意，我说年龄大了，能出站就很不错了。他也赞同，说我真是一个例外。

　　人生感言：引路靠贵人，走路靠自己，成长靠学习，成就靠团队。

　　I had my wish fulfilled.I came to School of Environment of Beijing Normal University and discussed with my professor about my study. According to their requirement，I should get at least two recommendation letters from major related professors. Besides my professor，another professor from the College of Resource and Environmental Science wrote a recommendation letter for me. Soon，I got the text message from the website. I went to Beijing to go through the procedure. I admired my professor´s judgement and told him the good news immediately. He was happy and asked me to do the research carefully and fulfill my desire. How lucky I was to have such a professor who understood me so well.

　　Soon after I began the study in the Post-doctoral Mobile Station of School of Environment of Beijing Normal University，my professor applied and filed for a 973 progress to be a young scientist. His graduate students were required to have one publication on foreign academic journal, which had at least 2. 0 impact factors, to get master's degree, let alone I was a post doctor. My professor sent two doctors to help me. Their specialties were related with my research area which made me feel more confident in Hydrological Model SWAT which was used on environmental science research.

According the requirement of the Post-doctoral Mobile Station of Beijing Normal University, I planned to finish it in two years. I should have two publications on academic journals and one publication on foreign academic journal with at least 2.0 impact factors. The papers to be published on Chinese academic journals were ready. There was no problem in submitting, accepting and publishing. What difficult for me was the writing of SCI. It went beyond my ability to publish on journals with at least 2. 0 impact factor. At first, my professor did not satisfy with several of my drafts. I always gave up and my husband convinced me to keep doing.

I searched online about the related English journals and learnt the writing skills from other scholars. One time, I asked the friend who helped me to transfer to the middle school of 104 Regiment for a help. Her Chinese writing was much better than me. I wanted her to review Chinese and then I could translate it into English. I told her I was frustrated because I could not hand in a qualified paper proposal my professor required. But she told me she could not help me because she knew nothing about my major. And she asked me to remember I need have the wings first before I jump off. I awakened suddenly and realized I only could rely on myself.

After that, I worked even harder. My hair fell seriously during that time. One year later, under the help of my professor and those two doctors, of course, also the support of my husband, the first draft of my SCI paper was finished. It got published half a year later. And I passed the report of finishing the research in the Post-doctoral Mobile Station. My professor tried to persuade me to stay one more

奥地利的蜗牛 (2017)
The Snail in Austria (2017)

year because I had the experience in writing SCI paper. I did not accept it. I was not young as other students and it had been the best for me to finish it. He thought I was an exception.

My experienced words: Helpful person guides your way, you go through it by yourself. Study makes you grow up and team makes succeed.

✳ 论文发表
Paper Publication

在博士阶段（2007 年 8 月—2010 年 6 月），我先后参加过国家自然科学基金项目"基于干旱区流域融雪径流形成过程及机制的大气水文模式耦合研究"（40871023）、教育部高校科技创新工程重大项目培育项目"新疆缓变型地质灾害监测、预警网络系统建设"（708090）、中国沙漠气象科学研究基金资助项目"积雪遥感与融雪洪水监测预测研究"（Sqj2007004）及新疆精河县、温泉县第二次土地调查项目。

发表论文如下：

1. 国外城市园林景观灌溉系统应用与实践 [J]. 新疆大学学报（自然科学版），2007，24（4）：464-467.

2. 基于 FAHP 原理的水资源承载力综合评价研究 [J]. 干旱区资源与环境，2008，22（10）：5-10.

3. 基于 SD 模型的博尔塔拉河流域水资源承载力研究 [J]. 新疆环境保护，2008，30（3）：4-8.

4. 面向生态的新疆艾比湖流域水资源合理配置模型探讨 [J]. 新疆农业科学，2009，46（2）：306-311.

5. 新疆艾比湖流域水资源供需分析与调控对策［J］. 冰川冻土，2009，31（4）：766-770.

6. 艾比湖流域水资源承载力综合评价研究［J］. 干旱区地理，2010，33（2）：217-223.

在博士后工作阶段（2011 年 12 月—2013 年 12 月），我先后参与国家杰出青年科学基金项目"生态水利"、新疆大学干旱生态环境研究所的国家自然科学基金重点项目"干旱区湖泊流域陆面过程及人类活动适应性——以艾比湖流域为例"及新疆联合基金项目"新疆博斯腾湖环境演变及对气候变化的响应"的研究工作。

发表的论文如下：

1. 西北地区某干旱河流设计情景下的年径流量预测分析［J］，冰川冻土，2012，34（5）:1236-1240.

2. *Relative effects of human activities and climate change on the river runoff in an arid basin in northwest China*［J］. Hydrological process. 2013. Published online in Wiley Online Library（wileyonlinelibrary. com）DOI: 10. 1002/hyp. 9982.

3. 基于不同盐度目标的湖泊需水量研究［J］，干旱区地理，2014，37（5）：901-907.

During my doctoral study, from August 2007 to June 2010, the researches I participated in were as follows: National Natural Science Foundation Project *Coupling Study of Atmospheric and Hydrological Model Based on the Forming Process and Mechanism of Melting Snow Runoff in Arid Region*(40871023), Major and Cultivation Project of College Science and Technology Innovation Project of Ministry of Education *Surveillance and Construction of Early Warning Network System on Delayed Geologic Hazard in Xinjiang* (708090), Funded Project of Research on Desert Meteorological Science *Research of Surveillance and Forecast on Remote Sensing of Snow and Snowmelt Flood* (Sqj2007004) and Project of Second Land Survey in Jinghe and Wenquan in Xinjiang.

Publications:

1. *Application and Practice of Irrigation Systems of Foreign Cities Landscape*[J]. Journal of Xinjiang University, Natural Science Layout 2007, 24(4): 464−467.

2. *Research on Overview of Carrying Capacity of Water Resources Based on FAHP Principle* [J]. Journal of Arid Land Resources and Environment 2008, 22(10): 5−10.

3. *Research of Carrying Capacity of Water Resources in Xinjiang Ebinur Lake Area Based on SD Model* [J]. Environmental Protection of Xinjiang 2008, 30(3): 4−8.

4. *Investigation on Configuration Model of Water Resources in Eco−*

oriented Xinjiang Ebinur Lake Area [J]. Xinjiang Agricultural Sciences 2009,46(2): 306–311.

5. *Supply and Demand Analysis and Controlling Countermeasures of Water Resources in Xinjiang Ebinur Lake Area* [J]. Journal of Glaciology and Geocryology 2009,31(4): 766–770.

6. *Research on Overview of Carrying Capacity of Water Resources in Xinjiang Ebinur Lake Area* [J]. Arid Land Geography 2010,33 (2): 217–223.

During my post -doctotal work,from December 2011 to December 2013,the researches I participated in were as follows: Funded Project of National Outstanding Youth Science *Ecological Water Conservancy*,The National Natural Science Major Project of Institute of Arid Ecology and Environment,XJU,*Land Surface Process and Adaptation of Human Activities on Lake Basin in Arid Region,Take EBinur Lake as an Example*,and Joint Fund Project of Xinjiang,*Environmental Change and the Response to Climate Change of the Bosten Lake in Xinjiang.*

Publications:

1. *Analysis of Annual Runoff Forecast of a Dry River in Northwest Under Designed Scenarios* [J]. Journal of Glaciology and Geocryology 2012,34 (5):1236–1240.

2. *Relative Effects of Human Activities and Climate Change on the River*

第 4 章

引 导 之 路

Chapter 4 A Guiding Way

Runoff in an Arid Basin in Northwest China [J]. Hydrological Process 2013. Published online in Wiley Online Library (wileyonlinelibrary. com) DOI: 10. 1002/hyp. 9982.

3. *Research on Water Demand of Lakes Based on Different Salinity Target* [J]. Arid Land Geography 2014，37（5）：901−907.

第 **5** 章　与众不同的人生

Chapter 5　Distinctive Life

智慧之人不以物悲，而以己喜。

He is a wise man who does not grieve for the things which he does not have, but rejoices for those which he has.

* 爱好广泛
Broad Interests

　　我家是个"象棋之家"，基本上每年都要举行一次家庭象棋比赛。我们兄妹几个从小受家庭环境的影响，都比较喜欢棋类活动，如象棋、军棋、跳棋等。父母比较喜欢下象棋，所以我们潜移默化地就学会了下象棋。父母的象棋水平相当，对弈有赢有输，母亲偏强些，估计是父亲有意让着她，免得自己没饭吃。哥哥们逐渐长大后也参与其中，我和弟弟紧随其后。不是谁下象棋的时间长，年龄大，谁就能每次胜利，而是师傅领进门，修行靠个人。我们同样被父母领进"象棋之门"，却是弟弟下象棋最厉害，每次获胜的概率最高，不服气也没办法，我是水平最差的，还比不过母亲，我可不是想让着母亲，确实能力有限！

　　母亲虽然从小身体不好，但是记忆力比较好。她可以做到每天晚上把当天老师的讲课内容在脑海中回忆一遍，所以成绩一直很好。她初小毕业，高中没有上完，因为身体的缘故，错过了考试，就不再上学了。她养好身体就参加了工作，那时也算知识分子了。我遗传了母亲记性好的优点，学习很轻松快乐，且从小在男孩堆里长大，颇有点男孩子的调皮劲。我兴趣爱好广泛，体育运动喜欢排球和羽毛球，棋类活动喜欢围棋和军棋，围棋在大学里研究了一番。学习科目我喜欢英语课和生物课。

我现在已年过半百了，这前半生过得可以说是有滋有味，酸甜苦辣都尝过。总体上，属于且累且快乐的人。当然是乐多于苦，因为我是一个乐天派。我始终没有放弃自己的爱好——英语。什么时候看到英文，都感觉很亲切，像见到亲人一样，真是一朵"奇葩"，这样描述比较顺应潮流。现在有各种各样的"奇葩"，各行各业，包括生活中，都不少见。我自认为自己是一个例外的"奇葩"，认识我的大多数朋友也这样评价我。

My family was called Chinese chess family. We had a family chess competition each year. My siblings and I like Chinese chess, army chess and Chinese draughts very much under the family influence. My parents liked to play Chinese chess, so we all learned to play it gradually. My parents were equally matched in their chess skill, but my mother won more times. We guessed my father lost deliberately otherwise he would have no dinner if he won. My older brothers participated when they got bigger. My younger brother and I caught up with them happily. The victory did not come with your age and how long you played the chess. It depended on your effort. My parents did not teach any of us specially, but my younger brother was the best in playing it. He almost won every time when he played with me. I even could not win my mother.

My mother was not in good health condition since she was little, but she had a good memory. She could recall everything her teachers taught during the day and remember them. She always had good academic performance. Because of her health condition, she missed the exams in high school and then she had to quit school. She went to work when she got better. And she was better educated than most of other people at that time. I copied my mother's good memory. Study was not a hard work for me. I was the only girl in my family, so I acted like a naughty boy sometimes. I had broad interests, for example, volleyball, badminton, Weiqi and army chess. A friend taught me Weiqi when we are in college. I liked English and Biology classes.

I am in my 50s, and my life was tasty and interesting. Generally, I had a tired but happy life. I believe I had more happy days than bitter days because of my outgoing personality. I never give up my interest in English. I feel warm whenever I read English. I am an exception in many people's eyes. There are many "wonderful flowers" in all walks of life. I call myself exceptional one among them, and most of my friends think so too.

*学会选择
Learn to Choose

　　人的一生中会遇到很多的"十字路口"，面临着各种选择，吃、穿、住、行、上学、婚姻、工作等，归纳起来主要就是工作和生活两个方面。我的高考经历告诉大家，高考让出10分的加分，是我不懂得选择，更不知道珍惜机会。性格决定命运有一定的道理，可是你可以改变性格中不利于发展的部分，扬长避短，有时候选择重于能力。就是说选对了平台，你的潜力有可能是你无法想象的巨大。

　　我的工作经历表明：有时候人要低头，是为了以后更好地抬起头；有时候顺其自然，有时候顺势而为，其实都需要我们的眼界和勇气。博士毕业后，我的博士导师首先给我推荐了一位北京师范大学的教授。我在网上查阅了他的相关资料，他的研究专业是水文学及水资源，与我的博士专业很接近。进博士后流动站要求跨专业，这点不符合。我考虑了很久，最终没有选择他。

过了几天，博士导师又给我推荐了一位北京师范大学环境学院的教授，让我与他联系进站事宜。我习惯性地在网上查阅了他的相关资料，发现他与我的老公同龄，立刻感觉很好。我进站后的研究方向是环境科学与工程，老公是做环境影响评价的，这也适合，而且可以发展我的水文模型 SWAT，三全其美，于是就选择了这位合作导师。随后，我就与这位合作导师联系，我们谈得很愉快，这就是正确的选择。

有人说，我们这个时代不缺机会，每个人一生会面临很多选择。那么，是遵从自己的内心，还是随波逐流；是直面挑战还是落荒而逃；是选择喧嚣一时的功利，还是恒久平静的善良。无论如何，希望每一个人，都能做出不让自己后悔的选择。很多事先天注定，那是"命"；但你可以选择怎么去面对，那就是"运"了。

You will meet many crossroads in your life, and you will meet all kinds of choice, for instance, food, clothes, house, transportation, study, marriage, job, etc. Mainly, there are only two most important things in your life, work and life. My experience of giving up 10 extra scores in final stage of high school proved I did not know how to choose and cherish the chance. It makes sense that personality is your destiny. But you can hide the disadvantage in your personality and make your advantage outstanding. Sometimes, your choice is more important than your ability. If you are in a right even better track, your potentials will surprise yourself.

My working experiences taught me that sometimes we yield for the purpose of rising better in the future, sometimes we let nature take its course, sometimes we follow the situation. Everything we do needs our courage and field of view. After I got my doctoral degree, my professor introduced me a professor from Beijing Normal University. I searched his information online. His research direction was hydrology and water resource which was close to my major. But they required us to cross major in the Post-doctoral Mobile Station. I thought it over and finally did not choose him.

A few days later, my professor introduced me another professor from School of Environment of Beijing Normal University and asked me to contact him about the details. I turned to search his information online and found he was the same age as my husband. I felt good immediately. My research direction would be environmental science and engineering and my husband's occupation was to do environmental impact review. That was suitable for me and I could develop the Hydrological Model SWAT at the same time, so I chose this professor to work with. Then I contacted this professor and we had a pleasant conversation. That was a right choice.

People say we are not short of opportunities in our time.

Everyone faces too many times to make choices. Then, we should follow our heart to choose or follow others blindly. We should face the challenge or be defeated and flee. We should choose temporary success or long-time peaceful kindness. Anyway, we hope everyone can make decisions in your life you never regret. A lot of things are predestined by heaven and that is the Destiny. But how can you make your choice is the Luck.

第 5 章 与众不同的人生 Chapter 5 Distinctive Life

* 幸运之人

Lucky Person

　　从五岁半上学当旁听生开始，我的运气就来了。我从一个旁听生成为正式的学生，在五连中学从小学顺利读到初中二年级。这其中有母亲的作用，因为她曾经是这个学校的老师。

　　初三上学期期中考试时，我家搬到了团部。当时，教我们的老师都是刚毕业的高中生，年龄比我们大不了多少。英语老师和数学老师都是女老师，很喜欢我，让我住在她们宿舍。她们担心我立刻转学过去会跟不上团部中学的教学速度，让把初

母亲在第七师 127 团五连学校留影
My Mother's Photo at the 5th Company School in the 127
Regiment of the 7th Division

三上学期上完再转学。都是为我好，我当然就答应了，况且"四人组合"的三个哥们都还在学校。

和老师住在一起，受益匪浅。近水楼台先得月，请教问题很方便，老师的参考书通常也可以借过来看。我有时还帮老师给差下生讲题和补课。我是学习委员，理应协助老师工作充当"小老师"。从那时开始，也许我就具备了当老师的潜质，只是自己没有放在心上，仅仅是当作一种体验和乐趣。

两个月很快过去了，期间，偶尔也会骑自行车回团部，看看父母和兄弟们。五连到团部距离不远，大概三公里左右，半个多小时就可以到家。初三上学期结束后，我办理了转学手续，依依不舍地离开了心爱的五连中学。那里有我快乐的童年和少年时光。非常感谢关爱我的老师们，向你们的辛勤付出表示崇高的敬意！

有幸赶上最后一批两年制高中，我可以提早一年上大学。虽然大学毕业时没有分配到理想的工作，但是却让我遇见了现在的老公，一个难得的四川好男人。

大学的姐妹情谊给了我实现梦想的平台，孩子的跳级和工作上的失意给了我实现梦想的机会和动力。从我在职硕博连读到进出博士后流动站，大约十年的时间里，始终有个默默无闻在身后支持我的老公。他懂我，知道我需要什么、想要什么，一直在物质上和精神上竭力相助。

从研究生到博士后，我先后遇见了硕士导师，博士导师——我的大学班主任，北京师范大学环境学院的合作导师以及两个优秀的博士，还有很多帮助我和支持我的师弟师妹们。一路走来，总是在走投无路时，柳暗花明又一村。就是这些亲人、恩师和朋友——我的贵人们，他们的无私相助成就了我的理想人生！饮水思源，我从心底里感谢生养我的父母，他们给了我鲜活的生命，让我拥有这么丰富多彩的前半生！虽然他们看不到我写的这本书，但相信他们的在天之灵会感到欣慰的，会一直保佑我继续前行！

I became an auditor in primary school when I was five and half years old, then my luck followed me. I turned into a formal student in that primary school, from then on till Grade Two in Junior high school. My mother played a part in it because she was the teacher in that school.

I had the mid-term exam in the first semester of Grade Three. When we moved to the regimental headquarters. Our teachers then were just some young people graduated from high school, and they were only a few years older than us. Our English and Math teachers were both female, they liked me very much. They allowed me to live in their dormitory. They worried I could not keep pace with students in the regimental headquarters, so they suggested me to finish the first semester. They were kind to me, so I agreed. The other reason was I did not want to leave other three of the Group-of-Four.

I learned a lot when I lived with my teachers. It was very

convenient for me to ask them questions and I also could borrow teachers' reference books. Sometimes, I assisted teachers to help some backward students. I was the commissary of our class, so it was my responsibility to help others. Maybe I possessed the potential of being a teacher from that time. I did not think too much about it and only considered it as an experience and interest.

Two months passed quickly, I would ride a bicycle to see my parents and brothers in the regimental headquarters from time to time. It was only about three kilometers from 5th company to the regimental headquarters. It took me half an hour to go home. The first semester ended, and I tore myself away from my old school and transferred to the new school. I had my happy childhood there, I felt grateful for the teachers and their heartful help.

How lucky I was to be a student of last two-year high school program, so I could go to the college one year earlier. Although I did not get an ideal job assignment on graduation, I met my husband——a nice Sichuan man.

Sisterhood in college gave me a platform to fulfill my dream. My son's grade-skipping and frustration in job activated the opportunity and energy to fulfill my dream. There were about ten years from my master and doctor study to research in Post-doctoral Mobile Station. My husband was always my strong support. He understands me well and he knows what I need and what I want. He supported me materially and mentally.

From postgraduate student to postdoctoral, I successively met my master professor, doctor professor who was also my college teacher, the professor from School of Environment of Beijing Normal University, two outstanding doctors and many other schoolmates who helped me. Every time I was driven into a corner, there would always be a way out because of my teachers, family and friends. Their help and love made my dream come true. I am grateful to my parents who give me life and give me such a wonderful life. They cannot read my book, but I believe they will be happy in the heaven and they will pray for me all the time.

四川成都的"墙景"
"Wall Scenery" in Chengdu, Sichuan

*计划与决定

Plans and Decisions

　　自从我懂事开始，就视母亲为榜样。我所有的好习惯都是母亲培养的，比如晨跑锻炼、做事有计划性、诚信待人、言出必行等。成家后，我的生活习惯就改变了，老公的生活节奏也是如此，就连怀孕这样的事都是猝不及防，还是年轻不懂事造成的。

　　有一件大事是我决定的，就是把孩子留下来。当时我们刚结婚，老公不太想这么早要孩子，说二人世界还没有过够。当时，学校有个语文老师，刚生完儿子，38 岁的高龄产妇，儿子是剖腹产生出来的。她年轻时一直怀不上，后来就抱养了一个女孩。现在女孩上初中了，她怀上了孩子，大家都说是这个女孩给她引来了孩子。她知道我怀孕后，劝我留下，她说第一胎的孩子聪明，要是打掉了，万一影响以后的生育怎么办。

　　听人劝，吃饱饭，我决定留下这个孩子。当时不知道是男孩还是女孩，我喜欢女孩，做梦都想生一个"白雪公主"。我怀孕后没有什么反应，还特爱吃甜食，吃蜂蜜都不觉得甜，好奇怪，别人都说"酸男辣女"，这爱吃甜好像没有什么说法。老公希望生男孩，因为他是家里的独子。我的胃口很好，不挑

儿子在西南交通大学的硕士毕业留念（2018）
My Son's of Master Graduation
Souvenir at SWJTU（2018）

食，肚子长得很大。刚开始还以为是"双胞胎"，做了B超才知道是一个孩子。由于我怀孕八个月时的妊娠反应比较大，地质队的医疗条件有限，队上医院建议我去乌鲁木齐大医院生孩子。

接着，我就联系了在乌鲁木齐军区总医院工作的大学同学，她父母都是军医，她在病案室工作，很快就安排我住进了医院妇产科。预产期到了，肚子还没有反应，又快到"六一"儿童节了，主任医生有可能不在，万一肚子疼就麻烦了，所以我做了剖腹产手术。1992年5月30日上午10点多，医生就把孩子从我肚子里取出来了，是个男孩子。躺在手术台上听医生说，这个孩子太嫩了。儿子嗓门还蛮大的，整个楼道都听得见，仿佛不愿意出来似的。所以这个孩子的身心都比同龄人晚熟些，现在也是一个硕士研究生了。

My mother was an example in my life since I was little. All my good habits were developed under my mother´s instruction， such as morning jogging, planning in advance, treating people with integrity and being a person of my word. My living habits changed after I got married and my husband had a same pattern with me in our life. It was unexpected for us when I got pregnant. It was because we were too young then.

I made a big decision that I was going to have this child. We just got married then and my husband did not want to have a child that early because he wanted us to enjoy the world of only husband and wife. I had a colleague, who was a Chinese teacher. She was 38 years old and she just gave birth to her son through cesarean section. She failed to get pregnant for many years, so she adopted a girl. She got pregnant when the girl turned into a teenager. People all said the girl she adopted brought the baby to her. She persuaded me to keep the baby when she knew I got pregnant. She said the first baby was smarter and it would have bad influence on my body to get pregnant again if I did abortion.

It is wise to take other's advice. I decided to have this baby. I did not know it was a boy or a girl, but I expected a girl. I dreamed to have a girl like snow white. I did not have much pregnant reaction. I still loved to eat sweet food. Honey is not sweet at all for me. It is said you will have a boy if you like to eat sour food and a girl if you like to eat spicy food. There is no saying for eating sweet food. My husband wished it would be a boy because he is the only boy in his family. I had good appetite all the time and my belly became bigger soon. I thought I had twins in

my belly, but the ultrasound told me there was only one baby. I began to have serious pregnant reaction in the eighth month pregnancy. The local medical condition was not good, so they suggested us to go to hospital in Urumqi to bear the baby.

Then I contacted one of my college friends who worked in Urumqi Military Hospital. Her parents were both doctors there. She worked in the Medical Records Room. She arranged me to live in their hospital soon. I did not have any reaction when the due day came. Children's Day was coming, and chief doctors might not be in hospital then, so I decided to have the C-section. 10am on May 30 1992, my son came to this world through C-section. Doctors said my child was so adorable. He cried too loud that everyone heard him on that floor. It seemed he did not want to come out. He was not a precocious boy compared to other kids. But I am still proud that he got his master's degree.

146

*亲近自然

Close to Nature

梦想已经实现，然而我却迷茫了。我能干什么工作，不知道，我处于一个尴尬的境地。回单位教书，不现实；换个科研单位，年龄又大了。真的到了一毕业就退休的地步吗？想一想，先放空一段时间，让自己的脚步慢下来，留出些时间看看风景吧！看看不同的风景，接触不同的人和事，你会发现，你的困惑是多么微不足道。

读万卷书，行万里路。教学这么多年，基本上都是纸上谈兵，世界这么大，我想出去看看。第一站，我去了老公的家乡天府之国——四川成都。成都的环境很不错，儿子在成都上了研究生，另一个家就安在了成都，我成了四川人。四川省地处中国的西南地区，位于长江的上游。成都到国内的东、南、西、北地区距离都不远，到国外也比较方便，开通了很多国际直达航班，交通很便利。成都的美食远近闻名，来到天府之国可以满足你的胃。如果是吃货的话，那可是来对了地方。

四川的山美水美人更美，可谓人杰地灵，川妹子个个长得很水灵。这里的生活水平偏低，物价也不高，人们很知足。所谓的知足常乐，四川人就做得很好。这里的生活节奏比较慢，

九寨沟风光
Scenery of Jiuzhaigou

人们喜欢打麻将、喝茶，生活比较悠闲。俗话说"少不进川，老不离蜀"，看来是有一定道理的。

山水如画的四川美景太多了，近处的有青城山和都江堰，远一点的有峨眉山和乐山大佛。我是地震前两年去的九寨沟和黄龙，不枉此行。九寨归来不看水，确实如此，说它美如仙境都不为过，真是美不胜收。地震后就不知道什么样了，所以说做什么事情都要宜早不宜迟，否则很多美景都可能被错过，何况人生还有很多其他的风景。

第二站，我去了海南岛，它位于祖国的南部，风景优美，物产丰富，是个旅游胜地。著名的景点如天涯海角、大小洞天等，人文景观也很多。旅行不只是看风景，更是给人带来精神上的改变。

I felt dazed after my dream came true. I did not know what I could do. I fell into embarrassing circumstances. It was not practical to go back to the middle school once I worked. And I was too old to go to a research institute. Could it be said that I would get retired right after I graduated? I decided to slow down my pace and space myself out for a while to enjoy scenery. To enjoy different scenery and communicate with different people will let know your confusion is not worthy of mention.

Reading thousands of books and traveling far. I had taught for many years, but it was always the empty talk. The world is so big, and I want to go and see. My first stop was my husband's hometown, Chengdu, Sichuan. Chengdu is a beautiful city. My son finished his master study there and our family is there now, so I become a Sichuan person now. Sichuan, a province in southwest China, locates in the upper stream of Changjiang River. Chengdu is not far from all directions of China and convenient to go abroad because of its developed flight system. Chengdu is also famous for its delicious food. It can satisfy all kinds of stomachs. It is the right place for all food lovers.

Sichuan has beautiful sceneries and more beautiful people. Girls in Sichuan are very beautiful. Living standard and prices there are below the average and people are content with their life. Sichuan people explain content is happiness well through their life. Their life rhythm is slow, they like playing Majiang, drinking tea and living a leisure life. It is said that the young do not go to Sichuan and the old do not leave Sichuan. It is reasonable.

Sichuan has too many picturesque landscapes. There are Qingcheng Mountain and Dujiangyan, Emei Mountain and Leshan Giant Buddha. I visited Jiuzhaigou and Huanglong two years before the earthquake. No water will be unique after you come back from Jiuzhaigou. It is as beautiful as heaven. I do not know what it is like now. So we should do everything sooner rather than later, otherwise many beautiful sceneries may be missed;besides,there are many other sceneries in life.

My second stop was Hainan Island, which is located in the south of China. It is rich in natural resources and has beautiful scenery. It is a famous tourist resort. There are ultima Thule and Daxiao Dongtian Scenic Spot and many other cultural attractions. Travel is more than the seeing of sights. It is a spiritual change.

美丽的大自然（德国）（2017）
Beautiful Nature(Germany)(2017)

* 珍惜回忆
Cherish Memories

　　回忆是对过往事物的遗留，尽管不再鲜明，却依稀可见，它们就像被封存在冰箱里、碗橱里的某些东西，静静地留在我们心灵的某个角落。

　　没有任何迹象，在我的父亲去世十年后，我的母亲在 2018 年 4 月 14 日突然离世了。让我意想不到，没有任何思想准备，忽然间一个大活人就没有了。我在母亲的家里住了七天，每晚都会醒来，朦朦胧胧中很奇怪怎么没有听到母亲的呼噜声，清醒后才知道母亲已经不在人世了。我心里很愧疚，以前不愿意与母亲同房睡觉，觉得她的呼噜声太大，吵得我睡不好觉，现在我想听也听不到了。感叹人生无常！

　　我们都有父母，希望大家在父母还健在的时候，好好地爱他们，好好地孝敬他们，不然等他们走了后悔都来不及。可能母亲是这个世界上唯一一个、我们可以不顾一切的、我们可以不顾虑任何的角色形象，把最真实的自己还原的那个人，还原在她的面前，可是我们没有考虑到她的感受。

　　生命，并不是你活了多少日子，而是你记住了多少日子，要让你过的每一天都值得回忆；人生的意义不在于长短，而在

父母在北京
My Father and Mother in Beijing

于过得是否有意义。生活如果能预知就不再是生活，就会变得索然无味。

我决定让母亲一直在我的生活中"陪"着我，尽管这听起来有点傻气，甚至还有些匪夷所思。但是，我要让母亲生前穿过的、摸过的、用过的东西环绕我。这就是我思念母亲的方式，这些东西让回忆成为一种爱。

做了这个决定，我懂得了在平凡的事物中也能找到安慰。

每天，我调动记忆里最高的幸福感用于现在的生活中，结果每天都能发现更多的幸福！总有一天，你的一生将在眼前闪现，请一定要让它值得一看。

有一种努力叫想改变，那是因为梦想的激励！有一种拼命叫我愿意，那是因为目标的动力！人的一生，最终你相信什么就能成为什么。因为世界上有最可怕的两个词：一个叫用心，一个叫执着。用心的人改变自己，执着的人改变命运。只要坚持在路上走下去，就没有到不了的地方。

最后，用一首英文歌曲作为这本书的结束语，它的歌名是《Dream It Possible》。表达出我对梦想与未来的信心与决心，并鼓励大家勇敢执着去追寻。梦想是我们的信念和精神支柱，支

152

撑我们走过一切困苦。想必你也会唱这首歌，这首歌就像为我
而写，同时也希望它为你而曲！

梦想成为可能

我奔跑　我攀爬　我要飞翔

我所向披靡

跳出我的桎梏　拨弄琴弦

是啊　我坚信

历史决定曾经　但并不能决定现在的你和我

所以我会不懈梦想直到梦变成真　直到看到漫天星光

不再畏惧跌倒　直到你展翅高飞的那一刻

当梦想成真　你便无可阻挡

挥着双翅　追随太阳寻找美好

我们会在黑暗中耀发光芒　点石成金

我们期待梦想成真

梦想成真

我们期盼梦想成真

我追随　我向前　我会展翅翱翔

直到跌倒　直到毁灭的那一刻

走出自我的牢笼　像黑夜中自由高飞的鸟儿般

我知道我在蜕变　在蜕变

变成未曾有过的强大

如果需要牺牲　需要无数的生命

那值得去奋斗

不再畏惧跌倒　直到你展翅高飞的那一刻

当梦想成真你便无可阻挡

挥着双翅　追随太阳　寻找美好

我们会在黑暗中耀发光芒　点石成金

我们期盼梦想成真

梦想成真

从低谷到巅峰

我们犹如燎燃的野火

永不放弃　永不退缩

直到我们生命的安宁

从低谷到巅峰

我们犹如燎燃的野火

永不放弃　永不退缩

不再畏惧跌倒　直到你展翅高飞的那一刻

当梦想成真　你便无可阻挡

挥着双翅　追随太阳　寻找美好

我们会在黑暗中耀发光芒　点石成金

我们期盼梦想成真

梦想成真

我们期盼梦想成真

Leftovers in their less visible form are called memories. Stored in the refrigerator of the mind and the cupboard of the heart.

Without any sign, ten years after my father's death, my mother passed away suddenly on April 14, 2018. I never imagined it and had no preparation for it. She disappeared from my life. I lived in her room for seven days after she passed away. I awakened every night and felt confused why I did not hear my mother's snore and then I realized my mother had passed away. I regretted that I refused to sleep with my mother before because I did not like her snore which made me sleepless at night. Now I miss it but there is no way to live again. How impermanent life is.

Everyone has parents. I hope everyone can love and respect their parents when they are still alive. Do not make yourself regret. Mother probably is the only person in this world who can accept the real us, no matter how terrible we are. We can do everything without thinking whether it is suitable in front of mother,but we never think about what she is thinking.

Life does not count by how long you live but by how much you remember in your life. The meaning of life is not the length of it but the meaning of it. If life were predictable it would cease to be life, and be without flavor.

I decide to let my mother accompany me every day in my life. It seems silly and unimaginable. I put all the stuff my mother wore, touched and used around me. This is the way I miss my mother, and these make memory a love to my mother.

My decision makes me understand we can get comfort in

normal things.

I put the happiest feeling in my life every day, then, I can find more happiness every day. One day your life will flash before your eyes. Make sure it is worth watching.

There is one effort which is called "want to change"as long as your dream encourages it. There is one effort called "I am willing to"as long as your target attracts it. You will turn into what you believe in. The most powerful words in the world are diligence and persistence. People with diligence can change himself and people with persistence can change his fate. You will arrive anywhere you want as long as you keep going.

At last, I want to end this book with an English song, Dream It Possible. It shows my confidence and determination in my dream and future. I encourage you to pursue your dream bravely. Dream is our faith and spiritual anchor,and supports us to endure all hardships. You may sing this song, it is a song for me and I hope it is also a song for you.

Dream It Possible

I will run, I will climb, I will soar

I'm undefeated

Jumping out of my skin, pull the chord

Yeah I believe it

The past is everything we were don't make us who we are

So I'll dream until I make it real and all I see is stars

It's not until you fall that you fly

When your dreams come alive you're unstoppable

Take a shot, chase the sun, find the beautiful

We will glow in the dark turning dust to gold

And we'll dream it possible

Possible

And we'll dream it possible

I will chase, I will reach, I will fly

Until I'm breaking until I'm breaking

Out of my cage like a bird in the night

I know I'm changing I know I'm changing

In into something big better than before

And if it takes, takes a thousand lives

Then it's worth fighting for

It's not until you fall that you fly

When your dreams come alive you're unstoppable

Take a shot, chase the sun, find the beautiful

We will glow in the dark turning dust to gold

And we'll dream it possible

It possible

From the bottom to the top

We're sparking wild fires

Never quit and never stop

The rest of our lives

From the bottom to the top

We're sparking wild fires

Never quit and never stop

It's not until you fall that you fly

When your dreams come alive you're unstoppable

Take a shot, chase the sun, find the beautiful

We will glow in the dark turning dust to gold

And we'll dream it possible

Possible

And we'll dream it possible